John Blackman was born in Melbourne in 1947 and began his showbusiness career in 1969 at Radio 2GN Goulburn. Since then, by his own admission, he's been 'through more stations than the Southern Aurora', including 2CA, 2UE, 2GB, 3UZ and 3AW.

During his 31 years in show business, Blackers has appeared in hundreds of television shows and commercials. He currently hosts a breakfast session in Melbourne on Radio 3AK and is in constant demand to compere awards nights, corporate functions and seminars, both in Australia and overseas.

However, he is probably best known as 'the voice' of Australia's highly successful and longest running variety show, 'Hey Hey It's Saturday', seen weekly on the Nine Network for an amazing 28 years. John, along with his many character voices and his alter ego, Dickie Knee, was a key component of the show since its inception in 1971.

John lives in Melbourne with his wife of 27 years, Cecile, and their 25-year-old daughter, Tiffany.

Also by John Blackman

Aussie Slang
Aussie Gags

MORE
aussie
GAGS

JOHN BLACKMAN

PAN
Pan Macmillan Australia

First published 2000 in Pan by Pan Macmillan Australia Pty Limited
St Martins Tower, 31 Market Street, Sydney

National Library of Australia
Cataloguing-in-Publication data:

Blackman, John.
More Aussie gags: over 1000 favourite one-liners
and jokes.

ISBN 0 330 36224 0.

1. Australian wit and humor.
I. Title

A828.802

Typeset in 11.5/14 pt Bembo by Post Pre-press Group
Printed in Australia by McPherson's Printing Group

Acknowledgements

Once again, I would like to thank all my friends (and the odd enemy), relatives, fellow performers and acquaintances for their contributions, inspiration and support in helping me to compile this second lot of one-liners and gags.

Special thanks again to my dear wife of 28 years, Cecile, who, whenever I began to flag from exhaustion, was right there behind me with a Bloody Mary (laced, I suspect, with amphetamines).

She's the only woman in the world who can make 'Good morning darling!' sound like a death threat.

May you enjoy many laughs.

Contents

Foreword

Congratulations on exhibiting such perspicacity, discernment and impeccable taste and judgement in purchasing this very rare publication, the last joke book I'll ever write (which is what I said after my first one).

But now, hot on the heels of the enormous success of *Aussie Gags* and under instruction from my bank manager, accountant and my wife or, as I call her, the Minister for Youth, Sport, and Procreation, here 'tis!

As the old adage goes, if you steal from one source, it's called plagiarism; if you steal from many, it's called research. Well, after months of 'research', I think I have now heard or read every worthwhile gag that's ever been written and stolen every one-liner that's ever been uttered.

You'll recognise some of the one-liners in this book as allegedly belonging to much funnier people than me and, under normal circumstances, I would ascribe: But (Your Honour and members of the jury), how do I know who *they* knocked them off from?

A pathetic excuse, I know, but it's also an environmental thing – think of the printer's ink and paper I'm saving.

Not all the gags and one-liners are laugh-out-loud

funny, but then humour is a very subjective thing and, as my butcher once said, 'One man's meat is another man's rissole!'

One thing you be can assured of is that every gag and one-liner in this book has been lovingly selected and road-tested on my wife, my mother-in-law (the Ayatollah), my friends, my vast radio audience (both of them), work colleagues and at many of the numerous corporate functions, awards nights, and conferences I compere each year across Australia.

In fact, I've just reminded myself of a guaranteed laugh whenever opening a conference, wedding or barmitzvah.

'It's great to be here at the Sunny Banks Function Centre. Coincidentally I was here just last week hosting a Gay and Lesbian Seminar; it's nice to see so many familiar faces back here tonight!'

Anyhow, enjoy this history-making book, use it wisely and, remember, laughter really *is* the best medicine. Use as directed and, if laughter persists, don't consult your doctor – just read the book again!

My Favourite One-liners

I just wish my kid would learn a trade, so he'll know, exactly, what *sort* of work he's out of.

People who give up smoking are just like nudists. They don't know what to do with their hands either.

I played a blank tape at full blast last night. Drove the mime artist next door crazy.

There are two things I don't like about my local member – his face!

He has all the sincerity of Colonel Sanders saying to a chicken, 'Trust me!'.

As Mark Twain once said, 'Statistics are like ladies of the night. Once you get them down, you can do anything with them.' He said it girls – not me!

When it comes to doing deals, he has a sixth sense. It's a pity the other five are non-existent.

If someone with multiple personalities threatens to commit suicide, is that considered a hostage crisis?

He has no life insurance. When he dies, he wants it to be a sad day for everybody – especially his missus.

When we were first married all we ate was toast – until she lost the recipe.

We've finally ironed out the divorce details – *now* she's ready for the wedding.

It was such a bad hotel – they stole *my* towels!

If olive oil comes from olives, where does baby oil come from?

Rough neighbourhood? We've got an Old People's Home that nobody ever makes it to.

When I was born, my father spent a week looking through my birth certificate for a loophole.

After eating, do amphibians have to wait an hour before getting *out* of the water?

A doctor gets to bury his mistakes. An architect can only advise his client to plant vines.

I told her I wanted to make love the old-fashioned way. She got me a date with her Granny.

I got an appointment at the Premature Ejaculation Clinic. As usual, I came way too early.

She's divorcing me because of my lousy memory. Every time I was near a pretty girl, I forgot I was married.

If you send someone Styrofoam as a gift, what do you pack it in?

Sharks never attack lawyers – out of professional courtesy.

Vegetarians don't love animals – they hate plants.

Never raise your hands to your kids – it leaves your groin unprotected.

Bad news: Her husband left her.
Good news: His clothes fit the new boyfriend.

My wife drives a lot more carefully since I told her that if she has an accident, the newspaper is going to print her real age.

I just put in a new skylight. It works great, but the bloke upstairs is a bit pissed off.

I asked my blonde girlfriend why she was staring at the bottle of orange juice. She said, 'It says concentrate!'

You know you're really drunk if you can't lie on the floor without holding on.

The sperm bank pays $100 per donation. Which means, I've let a fortune slip through the palm of my hands.

My blonde girlfriend's idea of safe sex is locking the car doors.

I'm having amnesia and déjà vu at the same time. I think I've forgotten this before.

Ever wondered why they sterilise needles for lethal injections?

My wife likes to talk to me during sex. Just last night she called me from Perth.

Loser? He carries around a picture of the model that came with his wallet.

Stupid? This bloke is depriving a village somewhere of their idiot.

Remember chaps, if sex using a condom is like taking a shower with your raincoat on, not using one is like having a bath with a toaster.

The best thing about his current girlfriend is that she has a beautiful face, a superb figure, never complains – and only takes ten minutes to inflate.

The recession doesn't worry me. I manage to screw up during the *boom*!

She said to the boutique manager: 'Do you mind if I try on that red dress in the window?'
He said: 'Sure – can't be bad for business!'

Ugly? Whenever she goes to the doctor he says, 'Open your mouth and say moo!'

There was this guy from Sydney whose watch was constantly running two hours fast. He couldn't fix it so he moved to Perth.

At the Paralympics, do non-handicapped people have special reserved parking?

Life in the fast lane can be very stressful – especially if you're driving a Lada.

I'm a sexual perfectionist. That's why I prefer to do it myself.

Politicians will find an excuse to get out of anything – except office.

The worst thing about being laid off is that, when you're taking a smoko, you're doing it on your own time.

Fact: Cannibals never eat clowns, because they taste funny.

The boss has just been charged by the police for molesting his secretary. He found out '*harass*' is actually one word.

Finding a needle in a haystack? No problem – all it takes is one match!

I asked my hairdresser what he would suggest to make me look younger. He said, 'Try hanging around with older women.'

Exclusive restaurant? The maître d' told me he'd have a table for us in about $20.

If a man talks dirty to a woman it's sexual harassment. When a woman talks dirty to a man, it's $5.95 a minute.

My golf is like masturbation. I derive a great deal of pleasure from it, but it's disgusting to watch.

You can't have everything – where would you put it?

I have to buy a new pair of glasses. I was kissing my girlfriend last night and she crossed her legs!

The boss asked me: 'How come I always catch you bludging?'
I said: 'Because you always sneak up on me!'

We were so poor that if Mum hadn't cut holes in my pockets, I'd have had nothing to play with all day.

Alcohol preserves everything – except your dignity.

Ever wondered why abbreviation is such a long word?

Big riot at the local prison – one of the inmates called another an insulting number.

When I die, I'm leaving my body to science fiction.

He didn't want his parents to die thinking he was a no-hoper. Fortunately, they lived long enough to realise he actually *was* one.

If you hopped into a cab and the driver started driving backwards, would he finish up owing *you* money?

That's all transvestites ever want to do: eat, drink and be Mary.

Alimony? Money that allows a woman who lived unhappily married to live happily unmarried.

I'm begging my wife to start having birthdays again. I don't want to grow old alone!

She's shy about telling people her age – about ten years shy.

I've discovered the secret of perpetual youth – lie about your age.

She asked me if I'd paint her in the nude. I said, 'OK, but can I wear a pair of socks so I've got somewhere to put my brushes?'

He's like a Scud missile in the sack. His aim's not too good and he goes off too early.

Do you realise that there are five syllables in the word monosyllabic?

She wouldn't have sex with him because she said she was waiting for Mr Right. What she really meant was Mr Bigger Penis.

He asked his mum where babies came from. She said, 'Ask your wife.'

I went on a crash diet and got down to my original weight – 6lbs 10 oz.

Love is blind. Well, someone's got to produce the ugly kids.

7/5ths of all people do not understand fractions.

The worst part about giving up cigarettes? Getting used to the ones your friends smoke.

Ever noticed that although he could stop bullets with his chest, Superman always ducked when someone threw a gun at him?

He's just seen his son's report card – living proof that the kid's definitely not using mind-expanding drugs.

Fat? If he's going to be home late, his mum leaves the fridge light on for him.

Inside some of us is a thin person struggling to get out – but she can be placated with a few pieces of double chocolate cake.

Drinker? He has Saloon Bar Arthritis. Every night he gets stiff in another joint.

He went to the cinema where the sign said: Adults $5.00, Children $2.50. He said, 'I'll have two girls, one old lady and a boy.'

Untrustworthy? Even the wool he pulls over your eyes is half rayon.

I get no respect from taxi drivers. Whenever I get into one, the driver leaves the 'vacant' sign on.

I told my date to make herself at home. So she rinsed out her pantyhose in the kitchen sink.
That wasn't so bad, but it was full of dishes at the time.

Waiter asked my wife how she'd like her steak.
She said: 'Medium rare.'
He asked, 'How about your vegetable?'
She answered, 'He can order for himself.'

He's been there and done that – and he's got the t-shirt to prove it!

Then there was the half-Irish, half-Italian girl – she mashed potatoes with her feet!

He told his teacher he was suffering from sexual exhaustion. She said, 'Try writing with your *other* hand then.'

Remember, it takes 42 muscles in your face to frown at somebody who's annoying you – but only four to extend your arm and smash them in the face!

Pathetic service? Next time I go to that restaurant, I'm reserving a table near a waiter.

I always drive with the handbrake on – that way, if an emergency occurs, I'm ready.

What do little birds see when *they* get knocked unconscious?

When I was a kid, I once swallowed a bullet. The doctor told mum to give me plenty of Laxettes and keep me pointed at the floor.

Dad showed me a picture of him when he used to be a boxer. If you turned it sideways, it looked just like he was standing up.

I got up this morning feeling like a million dollars – until I realised that was before tax.

Bumper Sticker: I owe! I owe! So off to work I go!

Death? Life's way of telling you you're sacked.

If at first you don't succeed, redefine success.

Note on door: Out to lunch – if not back by five, out to dinner as well.

Then there was the power blackout at an Irish department store – 40 people got trapped on the escalator.

Crook restaurant? I told the waitress my coffee was cold – she stuck her cigarette in it.

How come Tarzan didn't have a beard?

She's a great little housekeeper. Every time she gets divorced, she keeps the house.

Our school had a very strict dress code. The male teachers weren't allowed to wear them.

Most accidents happen in your own home. So I've decided to sell mine and rent it from the new owner.

Sex is not the answer – sex is the question. The answer is yes!

Whenever I read a good book, I would stop and thank my teacher. That is, I used to – until she got an unlisted number and a restraining order.

Democracy? Three wolves and one sheep deciding what's for dinner.

All the magazines in my chiropractor's waiting room are *back* issues. (Ow!)

Boring? At his last party his guests rang the police and begged them to come over and break it up.

He's a bilingual illiterate – he can't read in two languages.

Poor? My sister and I had to split a personality.

So if all those psychics know the winning Tattslotto numbers, how come they still have to work?

Then there was the blonde who got writer's block – taking dictation.

I used to work in a muffler factory – came home every night exhausted.

I told the boss, 'You can't fire me – slaves have to be sold!'

Every time I hit rock bottom, someone hands me a spade.

And that great Dean Martin hit: 'When you swim in the creek and an eel bites your cheek – that's a moray!'

Had a very busy weekend. It's amazing what you can do when your wife puts your mind to it.

Here's a sure way to get your spouse to pay attention and listen to every word you say – talk in your sleep.

Difference between a cactus and a school bus? The school bus has the little pricks on the inside.

She diets religiously. That just means she never eats in church.

Two fat blokes drinking in a pub.
One said to the other: 'Your round.'
The other one said: 'You should talk, you fat slob!'

What's better than roses on your piano? Tulips on your organ!

I'm leaving everything to my kids. I just hope they can keep up the repayments.

The difference between erotic and kinky? Erotic uses a feather – kinky uses the whole chicken!

The ultimate test of trust? Two cannibals having oral sex.

Cruel? He once bought a homing pigeon – then moved.

The truth never hurts. Unless you tell it to a really big, mentally unstable psychopath.

He's so impatient. He likes to leave phone messages before the beep.

He fell asleep listening to a learn-a-new-language record. It got stuck so now he can only stutter in Italian.

Ugly? His driver's licence stipulates he can drive only after dark.

I haven't been this excited since I put my underpants on straight out of the drier.

Pick Up Line: I lost my phone number – may I borrow yours?

Bumper Sticker: Beauty is in the eye of the beer holder.

Fat? He believes you should never eat on an empty stomach.

My wife said I should be more affectionate. So I got another couple of girlfriends.

If a man makes a statement in a forest and there isn't a wife around to hear him, is he *still* wrong?

As a wise man once said: 'A stigmatism is in the eye of the beholder.'

As another wise man once said: 'A fool and his money – get invited to an awful lot of places.'

Rough school? The kids had nicknames like Scarface, Slug, Dingo, Toilet Breath – and that was just the girls' netball team!

He's writing his first book. It's going really well – he's already got the page numbers done.

Cheapskate? On his wedding anniversary he took his wife out to dinner. But, as a special treat, he let her pick her favourite Hungry Jacks.

I am no longer confused about my sexuality. A woman I slept with recently said it was non-existent.

My accountant said I should diversify. So now I try to borrow money from a *different* friend each week.

My accountant has just changed his hours. They now run only 40 minutes.

We have a storybook marriage. Unfortunately it was written by Stephen King.

When I was 21, Dad finally told me where babies came from. But he never explained how the stork knew which house to go to.

He brings a new depth to shallowness.

He calls it puppy love. The RSPCA and police call it something totally different.

The cop said: 'Do you realise the speed limit is 60 kph?' I said: 'Yeah, but I wasn't going to be out that long.'

Rich? Her biological clock is a Rolex.

I'm a morning person. She's a night person. So we do all our fighting in the afternoon.

One good thing about putting on 25 kilos, you *do* lose your love handles.

Bad news. My boss wants me to re-locate – to another company!

You want sympathy? I once told my dad I had an earache. He told me, 'Use the other ear!'

My psychiatrist told me I was an obsessive-compulsive. Just to be sure I'm going to check – then double check! Then I might even just check again.

Idiot? He's just finished writing the world's first unauthorised autobiography.

The only thing I like about summer is that my cat loses hair faster than I do.

If your foot falls asleep during the day, does that mean it'll be up all night?

What a nightmare. He dreamt the plane was about to crash and the flight attendant still wouldn't give him her phone number.

What do you call ten blondes at the bottom of a pool? Air pockets!

All I asked her for was a simple massage. She said, 'Not tonight darling, I have a hand ache.'

I bought her a kitchen appliance that's cut her cooking time in half – an electric can opener.

We finally child-proofed the house. I went and got a vasectomy.

We have an open marriage. Every Wednesday she has a girls' night out – and every Thursday, *I* have a girls' night out.

He once held up a 7-Eleven. The shop assistant said, 'Are you serious?'
He aimed the banana at him and said, 'Does this *look* like I'm serious?'

He's so boring – even tele-marketers hang up on him.

He'd gone in for some cosmetic surgery – he swallowed a mascara wand.

Over the hill? The next time she'll have a firm body, it'll be the result of rigour mortis.

Eating out with the wife and kids? I call it 'whining and dining'.

I knew it was time to go on a diet when the flight attendant said I had too much carry-on luggage – and I wasn't carrying any.

Some major fast-food companies are using biodegradable packaging. Now if they could just do the same for their food!

If a slice of bread always lands butter-side down and cats always land on their feet, what happens if you strap some buttered bread on the back of a cat and drop it?

My wife almost had a terrible accident at the bank today. She got in the wrong line and nearly made a deposit.

I always leave my driveway at 100 kph. I have to – I live on a freeway.

When they got back to her flat she slipped into something more comfortable – a coma.

The best thing about turning 50 is that I'm now no longer prematurely bald (or grey).

Giving up the fags is not easy. When I go to restaurants, I have to request a table near someone smoking my old brand.

My accountant has a proven record. Three years in Pentridge and two at Long Bay.

And, as a wise man once said: 'Where there's a will, there's a lot of relatives.'

Things are so tight I've had to get a second job. Well, it has been a year since I lost my first.

I've discovered the boss and I have something in common – a pathological hatred of each other.

He puts his foot in his mouth so often he has to floss between his toes.

He was born by Caesarean section. That's why he always leaves his house through the window.

Then there were the two priests who went out on the town to celibate.

Her snoring is so bad that tugboats on the harbour have started answering her back.

For years I thought I had a club foot – until I discovered I had my boots on the wrong feet.

New Australia Post rule: If the package is marked 'fragile' it must be thrown underarm.

Little known fact: The ostrich is the biggest bird alive. It's also the biggest bird dead.

Q. How many Freudian analysts does it take to change a light bulb?
A. Two. One to change the bulb and the other to hold the penis – I mean ladder.

One good thing about a long engagement, at least it shortens the marriage!

It's always best to get married in the morning so if it doesn't work out, at least your *whole* day isn't ruined.

She's had so many facelifts, every time she raises her eyebrows, her pantyhose ride up.

Clever husbands always think twice before saying nothing.

And, as Jack the Ripper's mother once said: 'Jack, how come you never go out with the same girl twice?'

On our first date, she said she wanted to have sex in the back seat – while I was driving.

The first time she saw her husband he was outside Cash Converters picking his teeth – then he went in and bought them.

Low self-esteem? He threw a huge party – invited everybody except himself.

He's got a neat new job – narrating for really bad mimes.

Coming soon: The Dyslexic Theatre Company production of that wonderful Wild West musical, 'Annie Teg Your Nug'.

I tried to write a new drinking song but couldn't get past the first two bars. (Ouch!)

Jewish kid asks his Dad: 'What's two and two?'
His Dad replies: 'Depends son – are we buying or selling?'

Same Jewish kid in a maths class is asked by his teacher: 'Moshe, what's 3%?'
Moshe replies: 'You're right Mr Johnson, what's 3%!'

If you only have sex twice a year, does that make you bi-sexual?

If the pen is mightier than the sword, in a duel *you* take the pen.

My wife spent three hours in the beauty parlour yesterday – and that was just for a quote.

He was so lazy, he married a pregnant woman.

I've developed an attachment for my mother-in-law. It goes over her head and a strap comes under her chin to keep her trap shut.

He lost his job as a plain-clothes policeman because his clothes were just a little *too* plain.

The boss said: 'You should have been here at 8.30!'
I said: 'Why, what happened?'

Obesity is hereditary. It's when you swallow in your father's footsteps.

They say that every marriage is a lottery – but at least in a lottery you've got a chance.

What's green, has six legs and, if it fell out of a tree, would probably kill you? A billiard table.

Our local fire brigade has just bought a new truck. The old one will be used to answer false alarms.

I broke my mirror and got seven years' bad luck, but my lawyer reckons he can get it down to five.

Marriage? The price men pay for sex.
Sex? The price women pay for marriage!

I've got my nose to the grindstone, shoulder to the wheel, and my best foot forward – and I'm still broke! Who can work in *that* position?

My doctor told me the best way to overcome my flu was to stay off my feet and take plenty of fluids – which is pretty much a way of life for me anyway.

The difference between a breathalyser and your wife? Nothing – they both tell you when you've had too much to drink.

They say a nuclear war will be over in 20 minutes. Well at least that leaves your evening free.

What's the difference between a proctologist and a talk-show host? A proctologist only has to deal with one arsehole at a time.

She hates orgies. She never knows who to thank when it's over.

He loves the Stones. He watches them whenever he can. Fred, Wilma, Barney, Betty, Bam Bam, Dino . . .

There are only two things that have kept him from reaching the top of his profession – bad luck and a distinct lack of ability.

News Flash! Michael and Janet Jackson have both had sex change operations. They're now each other!

I asked the New York cop how to get to Carnegie Hall. 'Practice, practice, practice!' he said.

You know it's time to go on a diet when Japanese fishing fleets offer you money as a whale decoy.

I just got the results of my blood test. It turns out I'm senile positive.

Weird? He likes to go to topless bars and fantasise about what the girls would look like dressed.

Irishman walks into a bank, points his gun at the teller and says, 'One false move and you're geography!'
Teller replies, 'Don't you mean history?'
Paddy says, 'Now don't go changing the subject!'

I've been practising the limbo. I've become pretty good. I can now go under a rug.

My therapist told me there's been a big improvement since I started seeing him. He's just bought another Merc.

He's a real Do-It-Yourself expert – especially when it comes to sex.

That new waitress is great on the tables. Pretty good on any flat surface, actually.

Q. How many pessimists does it take to change a light bulb?
A. None. It's probably screwed in too tight anyway.

Q. How many male chauvinist pigs does it take to change a light bulb?
A. None. Let the bitch do the dishes in the dark!

Women need a reason to have sex. Men just need a place.

I said: 'I'll only put it in for a minute.'
She said: 'What am I – a microwave?'

Then there was the three-fingered pickpocket who specialised in stealing bowling balls!

At the casino I got into a raging argument with the girl at the roulette wheel over what I considered to be an odd number!

Sign outside Acme Radiator Repairs: A great place to take a leak!

You know you're getting old when you and your wife are ready to leave the house at the same time.

The horror movie was so scary, even the *married* people were holding hands.

Time to go on that diet when your tailor starts measuring you in longitude and latitude.

The four stages of old age:
1. You forget names.
2. You forget faces.
3. You forget to zip up your fly.
4. You forget to *un*zip your fly!

Reality? Waking up on your wedding day and realising you've just made 10,000 consecutive dates with the same woman (or man).

To him, group sex means using *both* hands!

You know you're getting old when you're dating someone half your age and you're not breaking the law.

Bargains at the Reject Pet Shop? A hummingbird that knows the words. A bloodhound with hypoglycaemia. A chameleon that's stuck on green. A depressed hyena. And an absent-minded elephant.

Skiing tip: You know it's frostbite when you take your gloves off and they're full of fingers.

Her cooking is so bad our Insinkerator has developed an ulcer!

Humour is contagious. Don't worry though, I'm not a carrier.

Show me a farmer who makes hay while the sun shines – and I'll show you a farmer with no headlights on his tractor.

His parents were heartbroken when he was born. There was a mix-up of babies at the maternity hospital and they got the right one.

Another way to reduce your cost of living – feed only your favourite children.

The difference between soybeans and vibrators? Nothing – they're both meat substitutes.

Advice: Never argue with your wife when she's packing your parachute.

I brewed some homemade wine. Had a strange metal taste – then I found my bridgework was melting.

The boss is a family man. But then, so was Charles Manson.

To overcome my insomnia I tried counting sheep. It was no good – I kept getting emotionally involved.

My shrink tells me I have low self-esteem but says not to worry. It's very common with losers like me.

You know you're getting old when most of your friends are anthropologists.

Chauvinist? He thinks brides only get married in white because it's good for the dishwasher to match the fridge and the stove.

Got a really cheap mobile phone from this bloke in a pub. Only a couple of buttons missing. It's great, except I can't call anyone with a 2 or a 7 in their number.

That's the last time I go to that fast-food joint. My hot dog had veins in it!

Fact: Frank Sinatra weighed 13 and a half pounds at birth – 12 pounds of that was ego!

My doctor told me I had the body of a 20-year-old – a 20-year-old *what* he didn't say.

My wife has the body of a 20-year-old – a 20-year-old Volvo!

He was born to work on radio – a 78-rpm mouth and a 33⅓ brain.

Girls, you know it's over if he's using your diaphragm as an ashtray.

When a man goes on a date, he wonders if he's going to get lucky. The woman already knows.

You know you're drunk when you feel sophisticated, but you can't say it.

He's got a tough job. Every morning he has to figure out how to look busy for another eight hours.

She once threw her panties on the stage at a Tom Jones concert. Problem was, she was still wearing them.

Adam was the first truly lucky man – no in-laws!

He ran the Ferris wheel and she ran the merry-go-round. Alas, their love was never to be for they moved in different circles!

As a wise philosopher once said: 'I had no shoes and I pitied myself. Then I met a man who had no feet – so I stole his shoes.'

As you go through life remember this: The caterpillar does all the work but the butterfly gets all the credit.

Saved myself a lot of money last Christmas. Told the kids Santa was in jail doing time for accepting secret commissions from Toys 'R' Us.

One good thing about being bald: When company arrives, all you have to do is straighten your tie.

How do you know you're at a Tasmanian wedding? Everybody's sitting on the same side of the church.

If you and your wife make a living selling marijuana, does all the money go into a joint account?

I've got something Kerry Packer hasn't got – no money.

So the experts say we're heading for a cashless society. Hey, I'm a jump ahead already – I'm cashless right now!

Then there was the heart-transplant patient who had a change of heart, and decided he didn't want a change of heart.

Drinker? He's the only bloke I know who blows on his birthday cake to light the candles.

Insult? Hey, great suit. How many girls you got working?

Tough suburb? The cats there had only six lives!

Special at local Mafia restaurant: Chicken Gangland –
chicken served face down in a shallow bowl of gravy.
Also, try our broken leg of lamb, crushed prime ribs and
today's special – stuffed turkey (stuffed with another
turkey).

You should always wait at least one hour before going
into the water after eating. Three days if it's my wife's
cooking.

The ideal gift for that lonely outdoors-type guy: A rubber
dinghy that converts into an inflatable woman when
you're out-of-sight downstream.

She was really in the mood for love. She hung a 'Do
Disturb' sign on her hotel room door.

I went to the drive-in in a taxi. Great movie but it wasn't
worth $157.00!

Beauty Tip? To look younger, try drawing smiley faces on
your liver spots.

Talking of that, cheer your priest up at communion –
tattoo a smiley face on your tongue.

He was so ugly, when he was born everyone in the maternity ward took turns slapping him.

Poor? Mum used to line our shoes with newspaper. She had to do the same thing with her bra!

My wife bought a flesh-coloured telephone so I couldn't tell if she was using it all the time.

He's so macho. He's the only bloke I know who drinks milk straight from the cow.

Then there was the blood donor who accidentally walked into the Sperm Bank and said, 'I'd like to give a pint.'

Adam: 'Honey, where are my pants?'
Eve: 'We're having them for salad tonight.'

I've got a great doctor. He soaks his tongue depressors in cognac.

We lived in a very small house. The front door opened onto the back porch.

The best part about being a new parent is that when you bring the baby home, it's already pre-assembled.

Marriage? A very expensive way to get your washing and ironing done for free.

The waitress said, 'That's not a fly in your soup – it looks like a whole pair of pants!'

Can a Rabbi ever become a *ham*-radio operator?

My teenage daughter has finally decided on a vocation. She plans to become an heiress.

My wife can press 80 kilos – and that doesn't even include all the wash-'n'-wear stuff!

When you're a young bloke, women tell you, 'Look but don't touch.' As you get older, you hear the opposite.

My old man told me to wake up to myself – so I've put a mirror at the end of my bed.

Had another ménage à trois last night – except the two girls didn't show up, *again*!

Went to a dyslexic drug rage the other night. Everyone was taking 'F'.

Did a stand-up-comedy gig at an old folks' home the other night. I wasn't very funny but they wet themselves anyway.

If every sperm is sacred, would that make his hanky drawer a temple?

Cop pulled me over for speeding on the freeway and told me I was stoned.
I said: 'What makes you think that officer?'
He said: 'Well, for one thing you don't have a car.'

The German word for father is 'farter' – which, in our house, is frighteningly accurate.

I've been blissfully married for seven years. Mind you, the first 20 were pretty bloody miserable.

What does an 85-year-old woman have between her breasts that a 25-year-old doesn't? Her navel!

You know the letter is from a leper when you find a tongue in the envelope.

Stupid? He's the only guy I know who went on 'Wheel of Fortune' and came away owing *them* money!

Our school is saving a lot of money by teaching driving education and sex education in the same car.

After he'd used up all his sickie excuses, he called in to say he was dead!

My wife always gives me half a bottle of whisky before dinner. She knows drunks will eat anything.

Did Mrs Arafat ever sing, 'Yasser – that's my baby?'

Ugly? Her appendix has been taken out more times than she has.

As a kid I remember sitting on that lap stroking that long white beard – geez I miss Grandma.

I never call out my wife's name when we're making love. I hate to wake her up!

The difference between a woman with PMT and a pit bull terrier? Lipstick.

Both my marriages have been disappointing. My first wife left me and my second one won't.

He owes his success to two main factors – hard work and that photo he's got of the boss giving his secretary a promotion on top of the photo-copier at the last Christmas party.

El Cheapo Airways? If you're feeling sick please use the bag the peanuts came in.

These days the only snap, crackle and pop I hear in the morning is me getting out of bed.

Life in the fast lane for him is the 'eight items or less' check-out at Safeway.

You know you're a bad cook when your kids ask to be sent to their room *without* dinner.

He always pays cash. Most of the women he meets insist on it.

He is one of the few people who actually look *better* in one of those Luna Park fun mirrors.

Touching storyline for my new movie: Boy meets girl; girl gets boy into pickle after boy gets pickle into girl.

Writing is: Simply stare at a blank sheet of paper until drops of blood form on your forehead.

God invented men because a vibrator can't mow the lawn.

Politicians? Classic example of why you should never shoot your mouth off without your brain being loaded.

Sunnyside Nudist Club is having their annual elections. Over 120 seats are up for grabs.

He won't be in today. He cut himself very badly this morning shaving and has had to go on Schick leave. (Ow!)

Men are like parking spaces. All the good ones are taken and the ones left over are handicapped.

I don't mind the missus being a back-seat driver, but I hate it when she sides with the police.

His breath smells like he just ate his track suit.

His breath smells like he just ate his underpants.

I suggested we do something different in bed. So she switched from 'Friends' to 'The Drew Carey Show'.

Farmer wins $10 million in Tattslotto. Asked what he'll do with the money he says, 'Oh, I guess I'll just keep on farming until it runs out.'

Very slow developer? He didn't have a birthmark until he was 13 years old.

Julian Clarey did s-s-s-*so* do National Service – the 125th Florist Regiment!

The difference between a light bulb and a pregnant lady? You can't unscrew a pregnant lady.

I am not considered a security risk. Nobody ever tells me anything!

A Port Douglas resort is so exclusive, the lifesavers won't rescue you unless you produce your room key.

What's worse than having your doctor tell you you've got STD? – your dentist! (Erk!)

Overheard at Muslim strip joint: 'Show us yer face!!'

The reason it takes 500 million sperm cells to fertilise one egg is because they won't stop to ask directions.

The three words women hate to hear when they're having sex: 'Honey, I'm home!'

One more drink and I'll be under the table. *Two* more, and I'll be under the host.

My wife wanted to discuss our marital problems. I said, 'You want me to turn off the footy for what?'

Poor neighbourhood? The local Salvation Army Band has only one cymbal.

The difference between a girlfriend and your wife? About 20 kilos.
The difference between your husband and your boyfriend? About 45 minutes!

Definite wanker? The only bloke I know with a five o'clock shadow on his palm.

I bought a car with a rear-mounted engine. Problem is, every time I stop too quickly, it falls off the back seat.

I'm a bit worried about my operation. I just saw the surgeon heating up some hot dogs in the steriliser.

The closest he's ever come to a ménage à trois is phone sex with twins.

His lips have never touched a drop of alcohol. Well, not since they invented the funnel.

Stupid? He's the Fred Astaire of foot-in-mouth disease.

Whenever he kills time, he tries to make it look like suicide.

I'm on a very strict diet. I now drink only low-calorie water – H-one-O.

Went broke. Invested all his money in air bags for dodgem cars.

The first time he had sex he got terribly confused. He didn't know whether to pay before or after.

He used to have a mind like a steel trap. Now, it's more like a sand trap.

He was a very good ventriloquist. When he died, the dummy did the eulogy!

She's stopped worrying now about her hair having body. She's more worried about her body having hair.

Inflation is really starting to grip. A picture is now worth only 800 words.

Got one of those cheap airfares. No stop-overs but you do have to change planes mid-air.

Yoga is not really helping her lose weight – but she can now eat in any position.

She only took up jogging so she could hear heavy breathing again.

Drunk? Wife wouldn't let me in the front door until I wiped my knees.

Etiquette tip: It's OK to eat a chicken with your fingers, but not while it's alive.

As the boss always says: 'He who laughs last gets sacked first.'

Good news: My wife wants to re-affirm her wedding vows.
Bad news: She wants to do it with her ex-husband.

The brain – what a wonderful organ. It starts working the minute you get up in the morning and doesn't stop until you get to the office.

He came from a very rich, dysfunctional family – born with a silver spoon up his bum.

Another way to get rid of all those wrinkles: Put on 120 kilos.

I'm not losing my hair, it's just moving to my back.

If you die before your time, how come you never get to go to your own funeral?

Marriage is not a word, it's a sentence!

I tried marriage once. Now I just lease.

My mother-in-law broke up our marriage. My wife came home early one day and found us in bed together.

He always wanted his name up in lights so he had it changed to 'Walk/Don't Walk'.

As a child I had a terrible fear of failure. I finally overcame it by becoming one.

Wives are so intuitive. I can't tell when she's faking orgasm, but she can tell when I'm faking an erection.

My doctor tells me I've got too much blood in my alcohol system.

Talking of which: 24 hours in a day, 24 cans of beer in a slab – too much of a coincidence?

He decided to become a chef to spice up his life, but unfortunately he just didn't have the thyme!

Then he decided to become a doctor, but just didn't have the patients!

Work is for people who don't know how to play golf.

I hate myself in the morning. So now I sleep till midday.

My daughter had her first sleep-over last night. Unfortunately it was with (insert least favourite football/basketball team here).

The Transsexual Society of Australia is about to hold its annual 'Come as You Were' Ball.

The latest dandruff solution: White suits!

Deprived childhood? When we went to the beach, my old man would slip the lifesaver $5 to keep an eye off me.

Husbands are like fires. They go out if unattended.

Get out! And never darken my bath towels again!

He has a nose like the legal process – long and cumbersome.

How unpopular is he? Debt collection agencies don't even return his calls.

After ten years I realised something was missing from my marriage – my wife!

The only reason women like the strong, silent type is because they think they're actually listening.

Tight? Bought his wife a new clothes dryer – ten metres of rope and two sticks.

Frigid? She could dry a wet floor by just looking at it.

I've just received some very disturbing news about my rich uncle – he's getting better.

Old? If I had known I was going to live this long I would have taken better care of myself!

I don't mind it when she laughs in bed. I just it hate when she points.

I became even more depressed when I found out how much I was spending on Prozac.

Ugly? Even the Optus girls say 'No' to him.

Boss's secretary has that sexy outfit on again. Last time she wore it, the sprinkler system went off.

We grew up in such a poor suburb, our rainbows only came in black and white.

He can talk for ages on any topic – even longer if he actually knows something about it.

I've discovered a great new diet. It's called poverty!

I lost control of my car the other day. The finance company re-possessed it!

Desperate? She had a prescription window installed for near-sighted peeping toms.

Definition of an unmarked car: One my wife hasn't yet driven.

Do not get in the car if his St Christopher medal is wearing a neck brace.

I'm the key man in our office. When the boss wants to go to the executive washroom, I hand him the key.

How hot was it? The thermometer said, 'Continued on the next thermometer.'

What does a blonde say when you blow in her ear? 'Thanks for the refill.'

Why does a blonde have TGIF printed on the top of her shoes? Toes Go In First!

Why don't blondes snort coke? The bubbles tickle their nose.

What does a blonde call brown hair dye? Artificial intelligence.

The reason husbands and wives don't understand each other is because they belong to different sexes.

Sex? The most fun you can have without smiling.

If it weren't for pickpockets, I'd have no sex life at all.

What did the blonde say when she found out she was pregnant? I hope it's not mine.

Favourite country song: 'If That Phone Don't Ring Then You'll Know It's Me.'

Drunk? The last thing I remember was trying to fit my car key into the Booze Bus cop's nose.

Went into an S&M bar and asked for a good, stiff belt.

Ugly? It's a face that could jump-start a lawnmower.

Ugly? He should have had his *face* capped!

Tight? He's not going to buy the Bible until it comes out in paperback.

The last time my wife and I showered together was when we washed the dog.

Poor suburb? We had to take our *own* books to read at the library.

Recent survey reveals 43% of Australian women know how to clean fish. Fifty-seven percent were too smart to admit it.

St Valentine? The patron saint of Hallmark Cards.

I've got to hand it to my missus – when she's right, she's always the first to admit it.

Tough school? After dissecting frogs in biology we were taught to wipe our fingerprints off the knife.

I am neither for nor against indecision.

I used to be indecisive – but now I'm not so sure.

If you eat enough natural, organic food you'll die a very healthy person.

Waddya get if you cross a pig with a centipede? Bacon & legs!

Ugly? She's cracked more mirrors than the San Andreas fault.

My great-uncle cheated the hangman. He choked to death on his last meal.

How do you change lead into gold? Ask a plumber.

The price of freedom is eternal alimony.

My wife's idea of perfect sex? Mutual headaches.

My doctor told me I was as fit as a Mallee bull. I'd feel better if I knew which end.

Sign on Australian Taxation Office door: 'Sorry – we're open.'

ATO mission statement: 'It is better to give than deceive.'

My psychiatrist has two baskets on his desk – one for 'outgoing' and the other for 'inhibited'.

She finally got rid of that terrible household odour. She told her old man to get out.

Cruel father? He used to measure my height by making a bullet hole in the wall above my head.

Ugly? They use her photo in prison to cure sex offenders.

Stupid? Obviously not a product of the MENSA Sperm Bank.

I only drink on rare occasions. Last night I had 14 rare occasions.

Time to go on that diet if you have to lie on the floor to zip up your fly (or, if you step on your dog's tail and he dies)!

It's easy to resist temptation. All it takes is a proper upbringing, a sound set of values – and witnesses!

She hated her last birthday present. Can't figure out why – it was the most expensive lawnmower in the store.

If it weren't for my wife, we'd be one of the nicest couples in town.

The difference between an anal and oral thermometer? The taste! (Yecchh!!)

I never underestimate my mother-in-law – unless I'm talking about her weight or age.

You know you're getting old when 'getting a little action' means the All Bran just kicked in.

The two certain things in life – death and taxes. Unfortunately, they don't come in that order.

I always try to pay my provisional tax with a smile. Unfortunately, the ATO prefers a bank cheque.

He's so juvenile, he even got his mobile phone from Toys 'R' Us.

Another way to drive somebody crazy. Send a fax that reads: 'Urgent – imperative you ignore previous fax.'

My secretary got her blouse caught in the fax machine – it ended up in Cairns.

Ladies, you know you're getting old when you try to straighten the wrinkles in your pantyhose – and you're not wearing any.

Dodgy restaurant? They honour Amex, Diners and Medicare cards.

Fat? He was the first ever test-*tub* baby.

Remember girls, the marriage certificate is a very important document. You can't get a divorce without it.

Tip for staying awake while on a long car trip: Drive with your finger in the cigarette lighter.

My wife wanted to spice up our sex life with some high heels, fish-net stockings, a garter belt and crutch-less knickers – but she couldn't find anything in my size.

Time to go on that diet if you get into a lift and you *are* the capacity.

He claims he'd never get circumcised because he'd have no place to put his chewing gum. (Erk!)

The only way he achieves 24-hour protection is to wear an odour-eater under each arm.

I had terrible trouble remembering names until I did the Dave Carnegie memory course.

I've just joined a no-frills introduction service. For just $5 they write your name on a wall at Flinders Street Station (or, pick one of your own stations).

We named our son after my father. We called him Grandpa!

Would a Mafia spaceman be known as a 'Cosanostranaut'?

Would a vet who teaches how to spay a cat be a 'neuter tutor'?

He wets his bed every night. Problem is it's from the top of the wardrobe.

He starts every day with a BLT – bacon, lettuce and tequila.

Ugly? She tried to trace her ancestors but the Kennel Control Council said their records were confidential.

He exercises religiously – every Christmas and Easter.

His breath was so bad the numbers fell off the thermometer.

He just got one of those $4 haircuts – a dollar for each side.

Did you know Dolly Parton has to cut her toenails from memory?

Miserly? He's ambidextrous – can't find his wallet with either hand.

I was educated at a Catholic school. The only one in our class with a moustache was Sister Bernadette.

He's a man of many parts – but then, so was Frankenstein!

Great salesman? He could sell nail polish to the Venus de Milo!

I've been smoking 40 a day since I was 16 and, you can rest assured, there's nothing wrong with *my* lung mate!

Uncle Harry finally stopped smoking – the crematorium just called.

Promiscuous? She's said 'yes' more times than Optus.

The Ayatollah Khomeini nearly died once after swallowing a beard ball.

Grandma has stopped wearing her hearing aid. She says she keeps hearing voices.

Premature ejaculation is hereditary because it comes in your genes.

As my good friend Wilbur once said, after I threw a golf club in anger into the bushes: 'I don't know if you'll find that Blackers – you'd better throw a provisional.'

Until she came along my life was empty – now it's my bank account.

Sign on lawyer's door: 'Suits Pressed While You Wait'.

Time was invented to stop everything happening at once.

A question that nobody's ever been able to answer: Were Fred and Wilma Flintstone married in real life?

I only realised she'd left me when I went into the bathroom, looked in the mirror, and saw a note nailed to my forehead.

At the Reject Pet Shop: A guard dog with dentures.

Graffiti: Atheism is a non-prophet organisation.

Bad personal habits? When he walks you can hear his socks crunch.

Her cooking was so bad the flies took up a collection to buy a new screen door.

That waterbed we bought hasn't saved our marriage. We've started drifting apart.

If marriage is an institution and love is blind, does that make marriage an Institute for the Blind?

Eighty per cent of men cheat in NSW. The rest cheat in Surfers Paradise.

Women's breasts are like electric train sets. They're meant for kids but it's Dad who usually winds up playing with them.

Sleazy? He's just been admitted to hospital where surgeons are attempting to remove a large breast from the palm of his hand.

Wanker? Surgeons are attempting remove his penis from the palm of his hand.

Eagles may soar, but at least weasels don't get sucked into jet engines.

George apologises. He can't be here tonight because his Granny is one hundred and eleven. (Wait for polite applause and then say . . .) 'Sorry – bad hand writing – his Granny is *ill*!'

I always borrow money from pessimists – because they never expect to get it back.

Harry is in a very sad and confused state – Queensland!

Brian couldn't make it tonight – but, according to his wife, that's the case *most* nights!

The problem with the gene pool is that there is no lifesaver on duty.

Sex on television can't hurt – unless you fall off.

My wife's writing a book. It's called, 'Women Are From Venus – Men Are Wrong'.

Dancing? A vertical expression of horizontal desire.

My wife's car has four headlights, two radiators and the engine's in the back. It wasn't always like that – only since she had the head-on!

Had a prang, but it wasn't my fault. I had the right of way, he had the cement truck.

Dad had an accident in his car. Nine months later there I was!

Tony will be a little late today as a result of a small collision. He was on his way to work when an original thought struck him.

I caught his one-man show last night. If you ask me, it has one too many cast members.

Bumper Sticker: To All You Virgins – Thanks for Nothing!

Bumper Sticker: Don't Be Sexist – Broads Hate That!

You know you're getting old when you no longer regard speed limits as a challenge.

It was a really moving performance. Everybody went home at intermission.

Then there was the Karate expert who joined the army and killed himself the first time he saluted.

He was always a man of action. When he was born he bungee jumped out of his mother.

He's kinda like Superman – faster than a tall building and able to leap a speeding bullet.

Got thrown out of the local bowls club for bowling over-arm.

People who know the difference between good advice and bad advice obviously don't *need* advice.

I always aim high. That way I never splash my shoes.

I have half a mind to get married. They say that's all it takes.

As you go through life, remember to look out for Number One but be careful not to step in any Number Two.

We made love with the lights on last night. She forgot to shut the car door properly.

One thing about old age, at least it doesn't last forever.

His sex life is so bad, he pretends he's drowning just for the mouth-to-mouth action.

Remember chaps, the only way to tell a woman's age is in a very low whisper.

She says she's 39. That's strange, when *I* was 39, it only lasted a year.

As Joan Collins once said: 'I love younger men. They don't know what they're doing, but they can do it all night.'

These days it takes me all night to do what I used to do all night.

He's so old, his passport photo was painted by Van Gogh (or, his driver's licence photo is in sepia).

The secret to a happy marriage? Never wake up grumpy. Let her sleep till you're out of the house.

We have a very balanced marriage. I tell her what to do – she tells me where to go.

I really surprised my wife on our anniversary. I actually remembered it.

After 28 years of marriage, I'm still in love with the same woman. I just hope my missus doesn't find out!

It's called a Pearl Wedding because, after 30 years together, you both feel utterly strung out.

I remember when my wife said, 'I do'. Unfortunately it was right after the priest asked if anyone present objected to the marriage.

If you come home to a warm kiss, a long cool drink, a sumptuous dinner and some wild love-making afterwards – you're probably at the wrong address.

Ahh love – the grout of wrinkles!

Carl Wilhelm Scheele discovered oxygen back in 1774.
Up until then we were breathing in any old crap.

He was so honest. At confession the priest would confess
to *him*!

Maths killed their marriage. She started putting two and
two together.

Bald? If he were a tyre, he'd be un-roadworthy!

Bald? He's got a receding hairline – all the way down to
his bum.

Wigs? He spent half an hour blow drying his hair and
then forgot to bring it with him.

Wigs? He met the original owner of his hair the other
day – one of the Carlton & United Clydesdales.

Wigs? Great rug – makes him look at least 20 years sillier!

Little known lost tribe of Israel – the Samsonites –
wandered the desert for 40 years with little food and
water but really neat luggage.

Then there was the Jewish mother who, every school holidays, would send her kids away on guilt trips.

I am an only child. My parents decided to stop while they still outnumbered me.

I was always a problem to my parents. Even as a kid I would bully my imaginary playmate.

What do Shakespeare and my parents have in common? They both know how to create tragedies!

They ran some tests on my wife for PMT. It turns out she actually never had it – she *always* been a bitch.

As a kid, I remember playing hide-'n'-seek with Mum and Dad. It took the private detective three months, but he eventually found them hiding out in Dubbo.

It's great being 52. In a few years I will have caught up with my IQ!

When I turned 50 I received half a telegram from the Queen.

Middle age? The first time you can't do it the second time. Old age? The second time you can't do it for the first time.

You know you're getting old when you don't have an enemy in the world – because they're all dead!

It's a fact that, at 80, there are six women for every man. What a great time in life to get odds like that!

Old? The State Emergency Service has just announced that the candles on Harry's cake are now under control.

I mean a lot to my parents. I was the son they never wanted.

Poor? My parents couldn't afford my 21st until I was 45!

Poor? When I turned 10 they put five candles on half a cake and put it in front of a mirror.

I've just joined the office Think Tank. It's great – we just sit around all day thinking and get tanked!

He doesn't have a drinking problem. He's actually donated his body to science and is simply preserving it in alcohol until it's time for them to use it.

When Pamela Anderson goes jogging, does she have to wear a chin guard?

The restaurant was so expensive my wallet got the bends.

My great-uncle died of asbestos inhalation. It took them two weeks to cremate him.

Bumper Sticker: Old Fishermen Never Die – They Just Smell That Way.

I'll bet you $100 I can stop gambling anytime I want.

She calls her wrinkles 'laugh lines' but, hey, c'mon – nothing's *that* funny!

Another thing to do on a quiet day: Stand outside the confessional and see which girl stays in the longest.

Frigid? She even gets a headache walking through Captain Snooze.

A question that has never been answered: At a lesbian marriage, the father of which bride pays for the ceremony?

My psychiatrist told me to avoid stress – so I stopped worrying about paying his bill.

My girlfriend saved my life in a restaurant. I was gasping, choking and turning blue. She saw what the trouble was and offered to pay the bill.

It's time to go on that diet if you have to drive with your car doors open.

I went to hospital once. Compared to the food, the medicine wasn't half bad!

I drive a two-tone car – green and rust!

He's so anal, he eats his alphabet soup in alphabetical order.

She's so anal, I got up in the middle of the night to go to the loo and when I came back, the bed was made!

They say truth is stranger than fiction. My wife says I'm stranger than both.

He does 50 push-ups a day. Not intentionally – he just falls down a lot!

Ugly? Child molesters used to knock on his mother's door demanding their lollies back.

He made a major contribution to medicine. He decided not to study it.

You know you're getting old when you can brush your teeth and whistle at the same time.

He only drinks to pass the time. Last night he passed 2001!

He drinks to forget. He drinks to forget he's an alcoholic.

Drunk? He once stuck 20 cents in a parking meter and, when the dial went to 60, he said, 'Crikey! I weigh one hour!'

He only decided to give up drinking when he saw the writing on the floor.

He once held up a ship launching for two hours. He wouldn't let go of the bottle.

An Amway salesman opens his door to a Jehovah's Witness – I'd like to see that!

Body-building couple broke up because his breasts were bigger than hers – but at least her penis was longer!

I finally stopped that door from squeaking. I locked it!

We were so poor, when I turned 21, they gave me the key to next door.

Their relationship failed because of incompatible star signs. She was a Libran and he was a dickhead.

It's time to go on that diet when you have more cleavage than your wife.

What a romantic night. On the way home, her head on my shoulder, someone else carrying her feet.

I've just joined Alcoholics Anonymous. I still drink, but under an assumed name.

I've tried the Drunk's Diet. It really works. I lost three days last week!

Remember, if you drink and drive you're putting the quart before the hearse.

I once downed two bottles of Johnny Walker and didn't even stagger. Actually, I couldn't even move!

Then there was the bloke who drank a bottle of varnish. Of course he died, but it was a lovely finish.

Molly Meldrum talks like that because, as a baby, his mother dropped him on his tongue.

In this computer age, the 'paperless office' really worries me. But not as much as the 'paperless toilet'!

Just got a bill from the finance company that said 'Final Demand!' Thank God for that – I was getting sick of them asking.

My boss says that 'Yes' men are pathetic, snivelling wimps. I couldn't agree with him more.

He looks just like his father, but that's OK – so long as he's healthy!

'Now, with what name do we christen this little boy?' asked the priest.
'It's not a boy, Father, you're holding my thumb!'

Last Christmas, Uncle Jeff took nearly five hours trying to stuff the turkey. In fact, he bloody near killed it.
Took us nearly all day to cook the bloody thing. Each time we put him in the oven, he kept blowing out the pilot light.

I once crossed a turkey with a kangaroo and got a bird you can stuff from the outside.

They made a fastidious couple. She was fast, he was hideous.

They married for better or for worse. He could have done better and she couldn't have done worse.

Did you realise that one in four people make up 25% of the population?

Dolphins are so intelligent that within just a few weeks of captivity they can train humans to stand at the edge of a pool and throw them fish.

Lady Godiva: The first woman in history to put everything she had on a horse.

A big cheerio to my Chinese dietician – Lo Fat.

Everyone's going too fast these days. On the Western Ring Road, if drivers are doing less than 110kph they get out of their car because they think they've stalled!

He keeps two sets of books. One for the ATO and the other for girls at nightclubs.

New theme park for the elderly in Surfers Paradise: 'Seizure World'.

They've actually been happily married for only two years – 1988 and 1994!

If a dentist marries a manicurist, when they argue, do they fight tooth and nail?

Sure my wife and I argue. Our most recent was just a little tiff – only three police cars and the Special Operations Group involved this time.

Remember, 100% of divorces start out with marriage.

You know the marriage is in trouble when she lines the bottom of the cocky's cage with your wedding photos.

The only time he ever got a standing ovation was when he addressed the Australian Haemorrhoid Association.

Doctors say sex is perfectly safe after a heart attack. Just make sure the ambulance doors are shut first.

I'm a bit worried about my doctor. When I dropped my dacks for an injection the other day, he dimmed the lights, put on some rubber gloves and started crooning, 'I'm In The Mood For Love'.

He's a great doctor though. If ever you find yourself at death's door, he's the one who'll pull you through.

Uncle Harry's a bit worried. Ten years ago he willed his body to science – they just called to say they need it tomorrow.

Patient: 'I think I'm going deaf Doc.'
Doctor: 'No wonder – you've a suppository in your ear.'
Patient: 'Thank God for that. Now, what did I do with that bloody hearing aid?'

Catholic Church just bought the local hardware store with a section devoted to DIT – Do It Thyself!

He left university with a Bachelor of Arts degree, a Bachelor of Science degree and a Law degree.
Unfortunately for him, they nabbed him at the gate and made him give them back to the students they belonged to.

When I was 18 my father sent me *abroad* to study. Boy! Did I learn some stuff from her!

Personally, I think all the fuss about dyslexia is a load of *carp*!

Then there was the nurse who thought she was so sexy, she'd always deduct five when she took a bloke's pulse.

Conceited? When he dies, he wants to come back as himself!

Dieting? Wishful shrinking.

Teaching is like acupuncture – one little prick after another!

A bachelor? A bloke who is footloose and fiancée free.

The three stages of marriage: The engagement ring, the wedding ring and then the *suffer*-ring!

This guy sings with all his heart and soul, and every fibre of his being. Just as well because his voice is crap!

In fact, last time he was singing 'Candle In The Wind', Elton John walked onto the stage and scratched his name off the sheet music.

Fat? She has so many chins, she needs a bookmark to find her necklace.

My wife had a very nasty accident in the kitchen last night. I think it was called dinner.

She specialises in Karate Cooking. She can kill a man with a single chop!

Her cooking is so bad the flies swat themselves.

Normally I hate to eat and run but, with her cooking there's no choice.

To punish our kids, we'd send them to their room *with* their dinner.

I'm a bit worried. The dinner guests we had over a couple of weeks ago are still sitting there.

Went to a weird religious restaurant in America. I got served by some Jehovah's Waitresses.

He hates drag races. It's just so hard running in a cocktail dress and heels.

Short? Gets all his clothes in a little shop in South Yarra – Dwarves 'R' Us.

They held hands all night. It was the only way to keep her away from his wallet.

Golf is a bit like sex. You always think you're going to do better next time.

That's the last time I take my bank manager to play golf. Every time I yelled out, 'Fore!', he yelled out, 'Closure!'

At The Reject Shop: A cuckoo clock where the bird backs out and asks, 'What time is it?'

I'm not an avid reader. Generally it goes in one eye and out the other.

I've only got two weeks to live. My wife's on holidays in Surfers.

I sent a postcard to my psychotherapist from Bali: 'Having a really great time – why?'

My son has just become a police reporter. Twice a week he has to report to them.

Eat a live cane toad in the morning – nothing much worse will happen to you for the rest of the day.

A tribute to my accountant Steve – a ledger in his own lifetime.

My Dad whacked me so often as a kid, I grew up with a cauliflower bum.

I was very different from the other boys in kindergarten. For one thing, I was 13!

Workaholic? His wife said, 'You spend no time with the kids any more.'
He said, 'Kids?'

Mum took one look at me when I was born and said to Dad, 'What will we call it?'
He said, 'Quits!'

Lawyers are like sperm cells. Only one in a thousand has a chance of becoming a real human being.

What do you call a bird that lies under oath? A Perjurygar!

Lazy? He can't stand seeing his wife slaving away in the garden – so he always closes the venetian blinds.

She married him as her partner for life then found out he didn't have one – a life that is.

Mother's Wedding Telegram: 'Twenty-three years ago I sent you to bed with a dummy. Tonight, history repeats itself!'

Our marriage is based on trust and understanding. She doesn't trust me and I don't understand her.

I have three dependants: My wife, my daughter and the Australian Tax Office.

I've met this nice German girl but our relationship is purely Teutonic.

Mean? His son asked him, 'Dad, if you had ten dollars and I asked you for two, how many would you have left?' His Dad replied, 'Ten!'

He started having sex with young women fairly late in life – like about three years into his marriage.

What a guy! Only 28 and already had five wives. Two of his own and three of his mates.

He's getting so much on the side he's started walking with a limp.

Promiscuous? She's seen more ceilings than Michelangelo.

Hey! Writing these one-liners is easy. All you do is laugh and then work backwards!

Rich suburb? So exclusive even the police have a silent number.
. . . and the Neighbourhood Watch is a Rolex!

Then there was the rich pig farmer who made sure every pig had his own pen – a Mont Blanc!

Then there was the day Kerry Packer went out and bought himself a set of golf clubs – Royal Melbourne, Royal Sydney, Metropolitan and Sanctuary Cove.
. . . and he cashed a cheque so big – the bank bounced!
. . . and he has three taps in his bathroom: Hot, Cold and Dom Perignon.

My ambition is to be filthy rich. Well at least I'm halfway there.

Actually, there's only one thing stopping me from being filthy rich. I don't have any money!

Once I went five days without food or drink. Then the waiter finally arrived.

I was a premature baby. Unfortunately I arrived three months before my parents managed to get married.

If there is such a thing as reincarnation, the boss reckons he's coming back as a human being.

Playing 'ships' with my girlfriend tonight. I'm going to be the *Titanic* and she's going to be the North Atlantic!
. . . then, we're going to play 'circus tigers' – she roars and I throw the meat in!

He never takes Viagra. That hour waiting for his erection amounts to some sort of commitment.

How come you never see women with 'Dad' tattooed on their arm?

Misogynist's Motto: Women only have orgasms so they'll have something else to moan about.

She said the most important thing in sex is foreplay. So he invited another couple around.

One thing not to say in a lingerie store: 'It doesn't matter what size – she's inflatable.'

Not much of a sex life. Spends most nights home alone playing strip solitaire.

Mum told me to eat my spinach so I'll grow big and strong just like Popeye. But she didn't tell me I'd marry a girl who looked like Olive Oyl!

Short? He used to milk the cows on his Dad's dairy farm standing up.

He comes from a long line of short people. His family tree is a bonsai.

What a fantastic variety concert – Barry Manilow sang, Jay Leno told jokes and Anthony Hopkins strangled a waitress and ate her liver.

The movie was so bad, the audience assaulted the usher.

He's a man of convictions, most of them overturned on appeal.

He's about as sincere as a hooker's orgasm.

He's eats a balanced diet – two Big Macs in the morning and two at night.

He's got a photographic memory. Unfortunately, he just ran out of film.

Golf? I spend so much time in the sand, I've been made an honorary general in the French Foreign Legion!

Golf? I spend so much time in the bunkers they've started calling me Hitler.

Golf? How did I play today? Had more hits than Elvis!

Golf? Lost four balls – and that was just on the practice putting green.

Golf? Lost four balls – and that was just in the ball washer.

Golf? The only two decent balls I hit all day was when I stood on that rake in the bunker.

Golf? Actually, my caddy says my short game is very good – especially off the tee.

Golf? What a terrible golf shirt – looks like something Cutter made when Buck wasn't looking.

Criminality runs in his family. He plans to follow in his dad's fingerprints.

At the Sydney 2000 Olympics they have introduced a new event to cope with the huge amount of drug testing – it's called 'Synchronised Peeing'.

He went on one of those 30-day diets; so far he's lost 15 days.

Sex is so much easier than billiards. For one thing, you don't have to chalk the end of your stick.

I've limited my drinking to one a week. I'm now up to July 14, 2003!

His serve is very hard to return – mainly because it never gets over the net.

Great tennis player? Her backhand was harder to get back than your virginity.

I nearly won a pile on this year's Melbourne Cup. There was my horse, right up there, alongside the winner – then the starter let them go.

They say that blood is thicker than water. I reckon he's thicker than both.

She was only ever unfaithful to him once – with the local cricket team!

Ugly? As a baby his mum would have to dip him in Whiskas to get the cat to play with him.
. . . or, tie a chop around his neck to get the dog to play with him.

He's got a good head on his shoulders. Now, if he only had a neck!

Blind date? She was a shocker. Sort of a Yasser Arafat with a blonde ponytail.

Burglar deterrent sign: 'Beware – Doberman bitch with PMT on premises'.

If a goose goes to a horror movie, does it get people bumps?

Behind every successful man is generally a very surprised mother-in-law.

Never attempt anything in the bedroom you can't pronounce.

I think about marriage a lot. It keeps my mind off sex.

Then there was the billionaire watchmaker who died. Lawyers say it'll take months to wind up his estate. (Boom! Boom!)

Then there was the Jewish Australian Princess who waited for years for Dr Right to come along. When she eventually did get married she promised to 'love, honour and oy vay'.

Never tell a surgeon, 'The way to a man's heart is through his stomach.'

He drinks so much scotch, Johnny Walker thought he was a wholesaler!

Fitness freak? He has a set of parallel bars at home – one for beer, the other for scotch.

He celebrated a double birthday recently. He turned 52 and his hair turned 29!

Guy to blonde: 'Would you like a Harvey Wallbanger?'
Blonde to guy: 'I'd prefer a drink first.'

Old accountants never die. They just lose their balance.

There are three types of accountants in life: Those who can count and those who can't!

My accountant is great. The ATO has just named a loophole after him.

Boring? When he was drowning, his whole life flashed before his eyes – and he wasn't in it.

It doesn't matter what temperature the room is, it's always room temperature.

Fact: Mrs Quasimodo used a wok to iron her husband's shirts.

Insignificant? When he walked into the room everybody thought it was someone important, but then realised it was a case of mistaken non-entity.

One advertising executive to another: 'G'day Bill. What's new and improved?'

The only place where success comes before work is in the dictionary.

His 1986 tax return was once nominated for the ATO Science Fiction Award.

Some Good Advice: Never argue with a stupid person. First they drag you down to their level, then they beat you with experience.

Some More Good Advice: Never wrestle a pig. You both get dirty and the pig actually likes it.

He's been described as sleazy, selfish, arrogant and untrustworthy and, let's face it, his mother should know!

I'm my own worst critic. My wife said, 'No you're not!'

My barman mixed me a strange new cocktail and called it the Autumn Leaf. It worked. I took one sip, changed colour and fell off the stool.

Lots of people have a wine with their evening meal – he has his with breakfast.

Then there was the National Dairy Milking Champion who shook hands with everybody – one finger at a time.

Boring? He's just been approved by the AMA as a sedative.

My wife and I make a great team. She does everything and I do the rest.

Fact: Chickens are one of the few things you can eat before they're born and after they're dead.

Arrogant? He was out taking a walk the other day and got hit by a speeding motor boat.

Is there another word for thesaurus?

She stopped after her fourth when she was told every fifth child born in the world was Chinese.

The difference between your boss and the Pope? You only have to kiss the Pope's ring.

She's been asked to get married hundreds of times – mainly by her parents.

Now look, if you don't like the way I drive, get off the bloody footpath!

If at first you don't succeed, pretend you weren't trying.

Some people leave a mark on the world – he left a stain (or skid mark).

Have you ever noticed when you pull a cat's tail, it's the cat that does all the pulling?

I suffer from 'alcoholic constipation'. I can't pass a pub.

As the private said to the general: 'Don't be silly sir. Those snipers couldn't even hit an elephant at this dist . . .'

I call my solicitor Rhino. He's thick-skinned, short sighted and charges a lot.

He spends so much time buttering up his wife, he's now got a cholesterol problem.

He says he only drinks that quickly because once he had one stolen.

In business, it's important you make your customer sit up and take notice – unless you're an embalmer.

He's got a stereo-sound system in his car – wife in the front, mother-in-law in the back.

Some of his school chums went on to become lawyers and politicians. The rest became useful members of society.

Egotistical? Only bloke I know who gives himself love bites.

Vain? He's got pictures of himself plastered on one wall – sober on the other.

Mean? At the reading of his will it started: 'I, being of sound mind, spent every cent I had before I died.'

Then there was the lonely contortionist who had a sudden heart attack and died in his own arms.

Then there was the lonely guy who was forced to have a ménage à moi!

Laugh and the world laughs with you. Cry, and you're probably looking at your penis.

My boss is a bit like Stonehenge – old, doesn't move and we don't know how he got into that position.

Had my cat neutered. He still hangs with all the other toms, but just as a consultant.

When he says his business is looking up, he actually means it's flat on its back!

Talk about a rough landing. I asked the pilot, 'Did we just land or were we shot down?'

Women's Weekly recently conducted a survey asking female readers if they ever faked orgasm. Thirty-seven per cent replied, 'Yes! Yes! Oh my God, yes! Yes!'

Big fire at the nudist colony. It took the members three hours to put the firemen out.

What's got four legs and an arm? A very contented pit bull.

They've started giving Viagra to old guys in nursing homes – mainly to stop them rolling out of bed.

She said when she dies, she's going to dig her way up out of her grave and haunt him. No problem, he had her buried face down.

He's about as popular as a piranha in a bidet.

Hooker to customer: 'It's a business doing pleasure with you.'

He really is in deep shtoop – he's even overdrawn at the Sperm Bank.

He suffers from paranoia and apathy. He knows people are out to get him but he doesn't give a toss!

None of the Collingwood (or insert suitable loser football/basketball team here) players are allowed to own a dog. For very good reason – they can't hold on to a lead!

In Los Angeles, if you want a breath of fresh air, you have to step *inside*.

His taste is so bad, his wardrobe is full of anorexic moths.

Hey, great suit! Nice to know Krusty the Clown remembered someone in his will.

I borrowed a book on improving your memory. I just can't remember who loaned it to me.

Q: What do you say to a cop who asks, 'Do you know how fast you were going?'
A: 'You should know smart arse, you pulled me over.'

My wife's favourite book is a cheque book. Once she starts one, she can't put it down until it's finished.

His suit is making a real fashion statement. I think it's trying to say, 'On him I look crap!'

Loser? For the past ten years, he's been riding on the crest of a slump.

Old? The best part about waking up in the morning is, waking up in the morning.

That joke is so old it was around when the Dead Sea was only sick
. . . so old, it was around when rainbows only came in black and white.
. . . so old, it was around when Mr Heinz had only one variety.

Pick Up Line Of The Month: Excuse me darling, I'm writing a phone book. Could I have your number?

Intellectual? Not only can he read the bottom line of the eye test chart, he can *pronounce* it (or, knows what it means).

There are two things I love about my job: Saturday and Sunday.

At my age I'm starting to appreciate the little things in life – like my bank account.

I complained to my lawyer about his fee. 'You ingrate!' he said, 'and to think I named my yacht after you.'

The shop said the jacket was leather. I said it wasn't. We took it to arbitration where the judge's decision was vinyl. (Ow!)

He has no luck with girls. Even Tammy Wynette refused to stand by him.

He's Scottish/Italian – pinches pennies and bums.

No frills manicurist: She *bites* your nails.

Inflation? Just when you're making ends meet – they move the ends!

Inflation? Where the buck doesn't stop anywhere.

Big eater? The only bloke I know who owns a wide-screen microwave.

As the wise guru said: You can pick your friends, you can pick your nose – but never pick your friend's nose.

He's bisexual. If he can't get it, he goes out and buys it!

The Diana Ross incident with security people at Heathrow Airport is a classic example of, 'Hell hath no fury like a woman scanned.'

Nappies and politicians should be changed frequently – and for the same reason.

The People's Republic of China recently ran a Best Political Joke contest. First prize was 20 years.

How many dyslexics does it light to take in a screw bulb?

When two opticians divorce, do they split everything 20/20?

On his birthday he takes a day off. On hers, she takes a year off!

When he was young, his heart ruled his head. When he was middle-aged, his head ruled his heart. Now that he's 65, his bladder rules *both*!

He's not going to be easy to replace because nobody actually knew what he did.

His wife does great bird impersonations – watches him like a hawk.

Kerry Packer is so rich he gets begging letters from the ATO.

Then there was the barber who broke both legs in a car accident and can now only cut hair on crutches.

Loser? Only bloke in history to be told by Mother Teresa to 'Piss Off!'

Bald? His hair is neatly departed down the middle.

I read all my contracts religiously – because the big print giveth and the small print taketh away.

Graffiti: Thank God I'm an atheist!

Actually, I stopped being an atheist because there were no holidays.

Dumb? He thinks Slobodan Milosevic is one of the Flowerpot Men!

I've just joined Alcoholics Unanimous. We still get drunk but we never argue.

The company secretary got sacked for being shy and retiring. The company bank account was $200,000 shy and that's why he's retiring.

If 15% of accidents are caused by drunk drivers then the other 85% must be caused by those bastards that don't drink.

My shrink tells me I've got a persecution complex. But that's because he probably thinks I'm inferior and more than likely hates my guts.

I told the kid: 'Don't be afraid, it's only an escalator – just step on it.'
He said: 'I'm not scared of it you idiot. I'm just waiting for my chewie to come back.'

I stopped drinking once – the most boring ten minutes of my life!

I've just joined Bachelors Anonymous. Every time I feel like getting married, they send around an ugly sheila in curlers to nag me.

I asked him why he was belting his kid. He said, 'He gets his exam results tomorrow and I'll be away interstate.'

The average Aussie kid watches 20 hours of television a week – slightly more when it's turned on.

There's nothing I wouldn't do for her and there's nothing she wouldn't do for me. That's how we go through life – doing stuff all for each other!

For 25 years, George and his wife were deliriously happy. Then they met each other.

I had my mother-in-law cremated and buried. Let's not take any chances!

The difference between a toilet and a wedding anniversary? None – men generally miss both!

My wife said she bought the dress for a ridiculous figure. I said, 'That's fine, but how much did you pay for it?'

Salvador Dali to Picasso: Excuse me Pablo, could I have a quiet word in your eyeball?

His bonsai tree business has become so successful he's had to move into smaller premises.

Bad gardener? He put in a rock garden and two of them died.

Gay? He even *walks* with a lisp!

Got two orders on my first day as a salesman. One to get out and the other to stay out!

He smokes so much, coughing is the only exercise he gets.

Cancer: Nature's way of curing smoking.

I've just been on a pleasure trip – driving the in-laws to the airport.

If we're not supposed to eat animals, why are they made of meat?

The sex was so good even the neighbours had a cigarette afterwards.

Diplomacy? The art of saying 'good doggie' until you can find a cricket bat.

Then there was the mute who swore – his mother washed his hands out with soap and water.

I went to a bookshop and asked the girl behind the counter where the Self-Help section was. She said, 'If I tell you that, it would defeat the purpose.'

Should crematoriums give discounts to burn victims?

Everyone should believe in something. I believe I'll have another drink!

My doctor gave me two weeks to live. I just hope they're in December.

Fact: For three days after death, hair and fingernails continue to grow. However, the phone calls start to taper off.

The difference between stupidity and genius is that genius has its limits.

Eunuch? A man who has had his works cut out for him.

Mothers are fonder of their children than fathers because they're more certain they're their own.

I have proof read this book thoroughly – just to make sure I haven't any words out.

In the end, everything is a gag.
Charlie Chaplin (1889–1977)

My Favourite Jokes

Elderly couple, who have been married 50 years, are revisiting some of the places they went to on their honeymoon. As they are driving through the secluded countryside, they pass a farm with a tall dingo fence running along the road.

The woman says, 'Darling, let's do the same thing we did here 50 years ago.'

The man stops the car, backs his wife up against the fence and they make love like a threshing machine.

Once back in the car, exhausted, he says, 'Honey, you were incredible! You never moved like that 50 years ago.'

She says, 'Fifty years ago that bloody fence wasn't electrified!'

'How come you're looking so glum today?' asked the geography teacher.

'I didn't have breakfast this morning,' mumbled Tommy.

'You poor love,' said the teacher. 'Well, let's get back to our lesson. Tommy, where is the French border?'

'In bed with my Mum – that's why I didn't get any breakfast!'

Wilbur and Ray are playing golf one day and Wilbur slices his ball into a deep, bushy gorge. He scrambles down the embankment and into the gorge to search for the ball. Suddenly, he spies something shiny in the thick underbush. As he gets closer, he realises the shiny object is an 8-iron in the hands of a skeleton lying near an old golf ball.

'Hey Ray, come here a moment. Quick!' he yells out.

'What's the problem Will?' asks Ray.

'You'd better throw me my 7-iron,' answers Wilbur. 'I don't think you can get out of here with an 8!'

Lifesaver walking along a beach one day hears a bloke, about 500 metres off shore, screaming for help. He dashes into the surf and swims out to the drowning man. Upon reaching him, he is dismayed to find the bloke has no arms or legs. So he hoists him onto his back and starts dog paddling back to shore.

Once back on shore, the rescued guy thanks the lifesaver, who seems stricken with pain.

The lifesaver says, 'I seem to have a really sore arse.'

'Yeah, sorry about that mate,' says the rescued guy. 'But, with no arms or legs – I had to hang on somehow!'

Two brothers were preparing to give urine samples after their respective Olympic events. During the procedure, the doctor couldn't help but notice they both had extremely long penises.

'How do you account for this?' he asked them.

'It's hereditary sir,' the older one replied.

'Oh I see,' said the doctor. 'Your father is the reason for your long penises.'

'No sir, our mother.'

'You idiot!' said the doctor. 'Women don't have penises!'

'I know sir, but she only had one arm, and when it came to getting us out of the bath, she had to manage as best she could.'

An agitated Olympic official was pacing up and down his psychiatrist's office, running his hands through his hair, almost in tears.

'It's terrible doctor – my memory's gone. I can't remember my wife's name. I can't remember my children's names. I can't remember what car I drive. I can't even remember where the Olympic Stadium is. It was all I could do to find my way here!'

'Now calm down,' says the doctor. 'How long have you been like this?'

'Like what?'

A good little Catholic girl, named Mary, kept getting into trouble at Sunday school because she had an unfortunate habit of falling asleep. One of her fellow pupils wanted to help and he asked his father what he should do. The father gave his son a safety pin and said to prick her every time she fell asleep.

That Sunday, Mary fell asleep just as the teacher asked, 'Little Mary, who is our Saviour?'

The little boy poked her with the pin and Mary stood up and screamed, 'Oh God!' and then fell asleep again.

The teacher then asked, 'Little Mary, who do we worship?'

The little boy poked her again and she yelled, 'Jesus Christ!' and promptly fell back to sleep.

Finally, the teacher asked, 'Little Mary, what did Eve say to Adam after they had their 99th baby?'

The boy poked her again and little Mary stood and screamed, 'IF YOU STICK THAT BLOODY THING INTO ME ONE MORE TIME I'LL BREAK IT IN HALF AND RAM IT UP YOUR ARSE!'

A young girl bursts into her parents' room just as her father is pulling on his underpants.

'Mummy!' she exclaims, pointing at her father's extremely well-endowed appendage, 'what's that?'

'Well darling,' says her mummy, 'that's your daddy's secret attraction. If it wasn't for that, you wouldn't be here today. Come to think of it, neither would I!'

An Olympic marathon-runner thought he would play a little golf to relax as he prepared for his big day. A golfer is standing on the 17th hole – a 170-metre par three with a 150-metre carry over a lake – rather than risk hitting a new ball into the drink – as he always does – he goes back to his bag and pulls out the oldest, rattiest ball he can find.

Just then, a voice from above – God – booms, 'Hit the new ball!'

Dumbfounded, he pulls the new ball out of his pocket and tees it up.

'Now, take a practice swing!' booms God.

He takes a practice swing.

'Use the old ball!' says God.

Bloke walks into a pub and sees a very attractive girl sitting at the bar. Summoning up all his courage, he goes over to her and says, 'Umm, err, is this seat taken?'

She responds at the top of her voice, 'You pervert! How dare you. No, I won't sleep with you tonight!'

By now, everyone in the bar is staring at them. The guy is totally embarrassed and confused, so he slinks off to a dark corner of the bar.

After a few minutes, the girl comes over to him and apologises.

'I'm sorry if I embarrassed you just then. You see, I'm a psychology student and I'm studying how people respond to embarrassing situations.'

To which he replies at the top of his lungs, '$200 FOR A BLOW JOB – YOU'VE GOT TO BE KIDDING!'

Young Ranald McDonald, champion Olympic hammer-thrower from Dundee, had been in the Olympic Village for two weeks when his mother came to visit from Scotland bearing all sorts of reinforcements, like whisky, haggis, salt herring and oatmeal.

'And how do you find your fellow athletes Ranald?' she asked.

'Mother,' he replied, 'they are such terrible noisy people. The one on that side keeps banging his head on the wall and won't stop. The one on the other side just screams and screams all night.'

'Poor dear Ranald! How do manage to cope with these noisy neighbours?'

'Mother, I do nothing. I just ignore them and sit here quietly playing my bagpipes.'

Bloke walks into the surgery and says to the doctor, 'Doc, you've got to help me. Some mornings I wake up thinking I'm Donald Duck and on other mornings I wake up and think I'm Mickey Mouse.'

'Hmmm,' says the doctor. 'How long have you been having these Disney spells?'

Elderly couple sitting in their rocking chairs on a porch one afternoon. All of a sudden, the old man reaches over and slaps his wife.

'What was that for!' she exclaims.

'That's for 40 years of lousy sex,' he says.

She doesn't reply and they continue to rock for a few more minutes when all of a sudden the old lady reaches over and socks him one right across the chops.

He says, 'Well, what was *that* for?'

She says, 'That's for *knowing* the difference.'

Elderly couple sitting on the verandah one night. All of a

sudden, she hits him over the head with a frying pan.

'What the heck was that for?' he exclaimed, rubbing his noggin.

'That,' she says, 'was for having such a small penis.'

A few minutes pass by when suddenly he whacks *her* over the head with the frying pan.

'What was that for?' she says.

'That's for *knowing* the difference!' he says.

A young couple arrives at the maternity hospital to have their baby delivered. The doctor tells them that he's invented a fantastic new device that transfers a portion of the mother's labour pain to the father. He asks if they would be willing to try it out and they readily agree.

For starters, the doctor sets the knob to 10% pain transfer, explaining that even 10% was probably more pain than the father had ever experienced before. As the labour progresses, the husband is feeling fine and he tells the doctor to bung it up a notch.

The doctor adjusts the machine to 20% pain transfer. The husband is still feeling fine. The doctor checks the husband's blood pressure and pulse and is amazed at how well he is doing. So, they decide to try for 50%.

The husband continues to feel quite well. Since it is obviously helping out his wife considerably, he encourages the doctor to transfer *all* the pain to him.

The wife delivers a bonny, bouncing baby with virtually no pain. She and her husband are ecstatic.

When they get home, there is the milkman – dead on the doorstep.

A 12-year-old girl comes rushing home from school and says, 'Mummy, Mummy, I just found out how you get a baby!'

'So, how do you get a baby?' asks Mummy.

'You get a baby when a man puts his penis in your mouth,' the little girl replies.

'Oh no darling,' says Mummy, 'that's how you get jewellery.'

Three women are sitting in the waiting room of their gynaecologist – the redhead and the brunette are talking.

The redhead says, 'I think I'm going to have a boy because I was on top.'

The brunette says, 'Well, I think I'm going to have a girl because I was on the bottom.'

The blonde girl suddenly bursts into tears.

'You poor dear – what are you so upset about?' they ask.

'I think I'm going to have puppies!' she sobs.

A young girl has just married a very big, burly bloke. On the night of the nuptials, she becomes very nervous and goes downstairs to her mother, who is washing the dishes.

'Mother, I just can't do it – please don't make me have sex with him!'

Her mother looks at her patiently and says, 'Narelle, it's your womanly duty – now go upstairs and everything will be OK.'

The daughter reluctantly goes upstairs where she finds her new husband preparing to undress. Removing his shirt, she panics at the sight of his chest hair. Running down the stairs she cries, 'Mother, mother! I can't! He has a hairy chest!'

Once again her mother replies, 'It is your womanly duty. Go upstairs and everything will be OK.'

Somewhat shaken, Narelle returns to her room to find her new husband removing his trousers and now sees that he has extremely hairy legs. She nearly faints and rushes back downstairs. 'Mother, mother! I can't! He's got really hairy legs! I can't go near him!'

Her mother, now really annoyed, replies firmly, 'It is your womanly duty. Go upstairs and everything will be OK.'

Trembling with fear, she returns to her room to find her husband removing his socks and realises, in horror, that one of his feet is half amputated. She runs down the stairs in hysterics crying, 'Oh mother! It's terrible! He's one and a half feet!'

With that, her mother throws down the dishmop, dashes past her daughter saying, 'Bugger it! *You* do the dishes – I'm going upstairs!'

Bloke walks into his doctor's surgery and says, 'Doc, my wife says I have a very serious sexual problem. She thinks I could be impotent.'

The doctor says, 'Mr Smith, bring her back with you tomorrow and let me see what I can do.'

The next day the worried patient returns with his wife.

'Take off your clothes Mrs Smith,' the doctor says. 'Now, turn all the way around. Lie face down, now face up. Now recline on your left . . . and right side. Hmmm, I see. OK, you can put your clothes back on now.'

Taking the husband aside, he says, 'Mr Smith, I'm glad to say you're in perfect health. She didn't give me an erection either.'

A chicken and an egg laying back in bed sharing a cigarette. One says to the other, 'Well I guess that answers *that* age-old question!'

Young bloke visiting a farm for the first time sees a rooster running around chasing after a hen. Just then, the farmer's wife comes out to feed them. The rooster immediately stops chasing the hen and starts eating.

'Crikey!' thinks the young bloke. 'I hope I never get *that* hungry.'

Bloke, giving a talk at his Rotary Club, got a bit carried away and banged on for over three hours. Realising what he'd done, he said, 'I'm terribly sorry I talked for so long. I forgot to wear my watch.'

A voice from the back of the hall piped up, 'Well you could have at least looked at that bloody calendar behind you once or twice!'

Young fellow asked an old, rich guy how he made his fortune. The old bloke put his feet up on his desk, put his hands behind his head and said, 'Well son, it was 1932, in the depths of the Great Depression, and I was down to my last penny. I invested that penny in an apple. I spent the whole day polishing that apple and, at the end of the day, I sold it for sixpence.

'The next morning, I invested that sixpence in six apples. I spent the entire day polishing them and sold them for a shilling each. I continued doing this for a month, at the end of which I'd accumulated nearly ten quid.'

'Is that how you made your fortune?' asked the young bloke.

'Not really, the wife's father died and left us $2 million!'

A young nun goes to confession and tells the priest she has a terrible secret.

'That's quite all right my dear,' says the priest. 'Your secret is safe in the sanctity of the confessional. What is your terrible secret?'

'Well Father,' says the nun, 'I never wear any panties under my habit.'

The priest smiles quietly to himself and says, 'That's not so serious. Say five Hail Marys, five Our Fathers and do six cartwheels on your way to the altar!'

'Great news, Mr Johnson. I think I've finally cured you of your kleptomania,' said the shrink.

'That's great Doc. If there's anything I can do for you, please let me know,' said the patient.

'Well,' said the doctor, 'if you ever have a relapse, I could use a nice portable colour television.'

A rich old man on his deathbed. Apart from the fact that he was dying, he was very unhappy because, no matter how hard he prayed, he couldn't take any of his wealth with him.

Suddenly, an angel appeared and said, 'I've just heard your prayers and had a word with the Big Fella. He said he'll make an exception in your case, but you're only allowed to bring one bag.'

The old bloke is overjoyed and orders his personal assistant to bring in a suitcase full of gold bars in preparation for his departure.

On reaching the Pearly Gates, St Peter stops him and says, 'Whoa there old fella. You can't bring that in here – you know the rules.'

The old man replies, 'It's OK St Pete, I've got special dispensation from the Boss.'

With that, St Peter opens up the case, takes one look at the gold bars and says, 'You brought pavement?'

B loke gets on a plane and sits next to a parrot strapped into the seat beside his. On take-off, he orders a cup of coffee from the female flight attendant, whereupon the parrot squawks, 'Yeah, and get me a whisky you fat, ugly bitch!'

The flight attendant, somewhat flustered, returns with no coffee but has remembered the whisky.

The parrot drains the whisky and squawks, 'Get me another one you fat tart, and make it snappy.'

'And don't forget my coffee please, miss,' says the passenger.

The flight attendant, now a little upset, returns with the whisky and forgets the coffee again. The bloke decides to adopt the parrot's approach and says to the flight attendant, 'If I don't get my coffee in the next two minutes, I'm going to give you a good kick up the arse you ugly, old trollop!'

With that, the flight attendant finally cracks and calls on two burly male flight attendants to throw both the parrot and the passenger out of the emergency exit.

As they're plummeting towards the earth, the parrot turns to the passenger and says, 'Hey mate, you've got a bit of an attitude for someone who can't fly!'

Businessman on a trip to Berlin picks up a hooker for the night and, after completing their 'business', he offers her $100.

'I'd prefer marks,' says the Fraulein.

'OK,' says the businessman. 'Eight out of ten!'

Harry the computer programmer, after 25 years of stress, decides to quit his job and go bush. He buys 50 acres as far away from humanity as possible. He sees the mailman once a week and gets his food supplies once a month. Total bliss.

After six months of this isolation, however, he starts to get a bit lonely. One night, there's a knock on the door. He opens it and there stands a huge, burly, bearded jackeroo.

'G'day mate! Me name's Bluey – your neighbour from five kilometres down the track. Havin' a party Saturday night – thought you might like to come.'

Harry says, 'Hey, that'd be great. After six months of this, I could do with some company, and it'd be great to meet some of the locals. Thank you.'

Just as Bluey's leaving, he stops. 'Gotta warn you, there's gunna be a lot of drinking.'

'Not a problem,' says Harry. 'After 25 years in the computer business, I can drink with the best of them.'

Again, Bluey starts to leave but stops. 'More than likely there's gunna be a bit of fightin' too.'

'Well, I get along with people fairly well so I don't think that'll be a problem.'

'OK mate,' says Bluey. 'One more thing, there's gunna be some wild sex as well.'

'Look, that won't be a problem, Bluey. Remember, I've been alone for six months. By the way, what should I wear?'

'Wear what you like mate,' says Bluey. 'There's only gunna be the two of us.'

The morning after their wedding night, the groom calls room service to order breakfast. 'I'll have three poached eggs, four fried tomatoes, six rashers of bacon, four hash browns, three sausages and two litres of orange juice.'

The operator asks, 'And what will your wife have Mr Rodgers?'

The groom replies, 'Just a head of lettuce thanks.'

Surprised by the disparity in the order, the operator asks, 'How come she's just having a head of lettuce?'

The groom says, 'Well you see, I'm conducting an experiment to see if she eats like a rabbit as well.'

Bloke walks into a bar and orders a double scotch. He downs it, and then pulls out his wallet and takes out a picture. He stares at the picture for a moment, then puts it back in the wallet and orders another double.

After downing that drink, he again pulls out the picture and examines it before putting it away and ordering another double.

This ritual continues for about four rounds of drinks before the barman asks him what's going on.

'Well,' says the drinker, 'this is a picture of the missus. When she starts to look good, I'm going home.'

Then there was the drunk staggering down the street with his car keys in his hand. He spies a cop and says, 'Hey, oshifer, you gotta help me. Someone has shtolen my car!'

The cop replies, 'Where was it the last time you saw it?'

'Right here on the end of thish key,' answers the drunk.

'Well,' responds the officer, 'you'll have to go down to the police station and fill out a stolen vehicle report. But before you do, you'd better do up your fly.'

The drunk looks down at his old fella hanging out and says, 'Oh my God! They've shtolen my girlfriend as well!'

A wealthy businessman on an interstate trip calls into the local whorehouse and asks the receptionist for the ugliest, worst lay in the place.

The receptionist is amazed and says, 'Sir, you obviously can afford one of our top-quality, highly skilled, beautiful girls. Why have you ordered the ugliest and worst girl in the place?'

'Look,' says the businessman, 'I'm not horny, I'm just homesick, OK?'

Then there was the 90-year-old man who streaked past two little old ladies sitting at a bus stop.

One old lady says, 'What was that, Mildred?'

'I don't know Gertrude but whatever it was, it needed ironing.'

Cop pulls a driver over on a country road. 'Do you realise your wife fell out of your car about ten kilometres back?' says the policeman.

'Thank God for that,' says the driver. 'I thought I'd gone deaf.'

A father and son are in the chemist when the young bloke spots the condom display.

'Why do these packs have only three in them Dad?' asks the boy.

'Well, son,' replies his father, 'they're for high-school boys. One for Friday, one for Saturday and one for Sunday.'

The boy picks up a pack with six condoms and asks, 'Why six Dad?'

'They're for university men, son. Two for Friday, two for Saturday and two for Sunday.'

The son then notices the 12-pack of condoms and asks the same question.

'Well son, they're for married men. One for January, one for February, one for March . . .'

Bloke rings his wife after winning $10 million in Tattslotto and tells her, 'Pack your bags. I've just won Tattslotto!'

Excitedly, his wife says, 'Should I pack clothes for warm or cold weather?'

He says, 'I don't give a stuff what you pack – just don't be there when I get home.'

Riding the favourite in the Melbourne Cup, a jockey was well ahead of the field. Suddenly he is hit on the head by a turkey and a string of sausages. Keeping control of his mount, he manages to get his horse back into the lead only to be struck by a box of Christmas crackers and a dozen mince pies. With great skill, he gets his horse to the front of the field again when he's struck on the head by a bottle of sherry and a Christmas pudding.

Unfortunately, he comes second, but he lodges a protest with the stewards claiming he had been seriously hampered.

'First,' said the office Romeo, 'I'm going to buy you a couple of drinks and get you a bit loose.'

'Oh, no you won't!' said the blonde receptionist.

'Then, I'll take you out to dinner and ply you with a few more drinks.'

'Oh, no you won't,' she says.

'Then I'll take you to my apartment and keep serving you drinks.'

'Oh, no you won't.'

'Then, I'm going to make violent, passionate love to you.'

'Oh, no you won't,' she says.

'And, I'm not going to wear a condom either!' says Romeo.

'Oh, yes you will!' says the girl.

A blonde girl's car gets caught in a violent hailstorm. After checking, she finds her car is covered in rather large dents. She takes it to the local panel beater to find out how to fix the problem. The panel beater tells her, with a smirk, to blow into the exhaust pipe and the dents will pop out.

But as she is doing this, another blonde walks past and asks her what she is doing. The first blonde tells her, to which the second blonde responds, 'Well, that's pretty silly. It'll only work if you wind up the windows first.'

An Englishman, a German, a Scotsman and an Irishman were sitting around the lunchroom discussing how stupid their wives are. The Englishman says, 'My wife is so stupid. Last week she went and bought $400 worth of meat which was on special and we don't even own a freezer!'

'That's nothing,' says the German. 'My wife just bought $2000 worth of ski gear and she can't even ski.'

'I can top that!' pipes up the Scotsman. 'My wife is as thick as two short planks. Last week she went out and bought a $45,000 sports car, and she's never driven in her life.'

The Irishman starts laughing out loud and says, 'You're all very lucky. My wife is so stupid, on her last trip to Greece, I watched her packing her bag. She must have put about 200 condoms in there and she doesn't even have a penis!'

Two mates playing golf together. One of them has a little Jack Russell terrier with him and, every time he sinks a 20-metre putt, the dog yips and prances around the green on his hind legs.

'That's incredible Harry. What does he do if you miss a putt?' asks his golfing companion.

'Somersaults,' says his mate.

'Somersaults?' says his friend. 'That's amazing. How many does he do?'

'Depends on how hard I foot him up the arse!'

A blonde and a lawyer are seated next to each other on a flight from Melbourne to Perth. Knowing it was going to be a very long journey, the lawyer asks the blonde if she'd like to play a mind game, which was easy and a lot of fun. Reluctantly, the blonde girl agrees.

The lawyer tells her the rules.

'I ask you a question and if you don't know the answer, you pay me $5 and if I don't know the answer I'll pay you $500!'

Then he asks the first question. 'What's the distance from Earth to the moon?'

The blonde doesn't say a word, reaches into her purse and hands the lawyer $5.

'OK,' says the lawyer, 'your turn.'

So the blonde asks the lawyer, 'What goes up a hill with three legs and comes down with four?'

The lawyer, totally puzzled, pulls out his lap-top and searches for any possible links – nothing. Frustrated, he illegally uses his mobile phone in the toilet, phoning friends all over the country – still nothing. An hour later, totally beaten, he hands the blonde $500.

'Thank you,' she says, and she turns over to have a snooze.

An hour later, the lawyer wakes the blonde and asks, 'Well, what's the answer?'

Without a word, the blonde reaches into her purse, hands the lawyer $5 and goes back to sleep.

A few minutes before the famous Shakespearian actor, Douglas Fairfax, was about to perform Macbeth before a packed theatre audience in New York, he had a heart attack and dropped dead. The stage manager solemnly came onstage and announced: 'We are very sorry to bring this news. Mr Douglas Fairfax Jr has sadly passed away in his dressing room and there will be no performance tonight.'

From the back stalls a voice cried out, 'Give him some chicken soup!'

Quite startled, the stage manager clears his throat and said, 'I apologise if, in my grief, I have not made my solemn message clear. Mr Fairfax Jr is deceased and there will be no performance.'

Again, from the back stalls, the voice called out, 'Give him some chicken soup!'

Impatiently, the manager yelled back, 'Lady, the man is dead. Giving him some chicken soup couldn't help.'

The voice replied, 'It couldn't hurt!'

An elderly old guy shuffles into his doctor's surgery in great pain. With a great deal of embarrassment he tells the doctor that his penis is very, very sore and tender.

'It's the missus Doc,' the old guy says. 'You see, last night she dreamt she was playing the pokies and my old fella was the lever.'

'Good grief!' said the doctor. 'Why didn't you say something?'

'I couldn't, Doc. I had a mouthful of ten cent pieces!'

Couple in restaurant gazing into each other's eyes – obviously in love. Just as the woman glances away for a moment, the waitress comes rushing over.

'Excuse me madam, but your husband's just slid under the table!'

'Oh no he didn't,' the woman replies. 'My husband just came in the door!'

Little Italian guy enters the witness box, very nervously takes the oath, and gazes around with a great deal of anxiety, overawed by the enormity of the occasion.

The police prosecutor asks, 'Are you Giovanni Pasquale?'

'Yes,' replies the witness.

'And you live at 345 Smith Street, Thomastown?'

'Yes, I do.'

'And you're a waiter?'

'Seventy kilos!'

Paddy McGuiness is digging a hole when the local constable approaches.

'What are you doing?' inquires the policeman.

'I'm digging a hole to bury me dog, sir,' says Paddy.

'Well, what are those other three holes for then?' asks the cop.

'Well sir, they were going to be for the dog, but they weren't big enough.'

There they are on the sofa, making mad, passionate love when the phone rings. Within a minute, she's back.

'Who was that?' he asks.

'That was my husband,' she replies.

'Crikey!' he exclaims, 'I'd better get out of here.'

'Relax darling,' she says. 'He's in town playing poker with you.'

Bloke goes into his doctor and says, 'Doc, I've got a cricket ball up me bum!'

'Howzat!' says the doctor.

'Now don't you bloody start!' says the patient.

Bloke goes into his doctor and says, 'I keep hearing these two songs – "Delilah" and "The Green Green Grass of Home".'

'Hmmm,' says the Doc. 'Sounds like you've got Tom Jones Syndrome.'

'Is it common?' asks the patient.

'"It's Not Unusual",' sings the doctor.

Bloke takes his Labrador to the vet. 'My dog's cross-eyed. Is there anything you can do for him Doc?'

'Hmmm, let's take a look at him,' says the vet. The vet picks up the dog by the ears and takes a good long hard look at his eyes.

'Well,' says the vet, 'I'm afraid I'm going to have to put him down.'

'Why? Just because he's cross-eyed?'

'No – because he's heavy.'

And now, a lovely little gag for you sensitive new age guys out there.

Bloke sitting in an aluminium lawn chair one Sunday afternoon, sipping a beer and watching his wife mow the lawn. Outraged, the lady next door storms over the fence and starts shouting at him.

'You should be *hung*, well and truly!' she berates.

'I *am*,' he says. 'That's why she cuts the grass.'

Duck walks into a bar and orders a beer. The barman is amazed. 'Hey, you're a duck that can talk!' he exclaims.

'Very observant of you old boy,' says the duck. 'Now, I'll be working on that building site across the road for the next couple of weeks and I'll be in each lunch time for a pot of beer.'

So, each day, the duck waddles in and downs a pot of beer then goes back to the building site. One day, the barman says to the duck, 'You know the circus has just arrived in town and I was talking to the owner about you and he's very interested.'

'Really?' says the duck.

'Straight up,' says the barman. 'And you could make a lot of money. I can tee it up for you no worries.'

'Hang on,' says the duck. 'You said *circus*, didn't you?'

'That's right,' says the barman.

'One of those big tent things with a pole up the middle?'

'Yeah,' says the barman.

'Made out of canvas, right?' says the duck.

'Yeah, yeah, canvas,' says the barman getting very excited. 'I can get you started tomorrow. The circus owner's dead keen.'

Looking quite puzzled, the duck scratches his bill and says, 'Can't understand what the hell he wants me for – I'm a plasterer.'

An archaeologist, digging in a desert in Israel, comes across a casket containing a mummy. Very excited, he transports it to a prestigious natural history museum for detailed analysis. A few weeks later, he gets a call from the curator.

'That mummy you brought in – it's 3000 years old and died of heart failure,' the curator informs him.

'Heart failure?' says the archaeologist. 'How can you be so certain?'

'Easy. We found a piece of papyrus in his hand that said, "100,000 shekels on Goliath".'

Four golfers are putting out when they see a lone player behind them play up short and hurriedly chip up onto their green.

'I say chaps,' pants the lone golfer, 'do you mind if I play through?'

'Not at all,' they say, 'but what's the big hurry?'

'The hospital's just phoned. The wife's been in a

terrible car accident and she's not expected to survive the afternoon.'

Old guy walks into a crowded doctor's waiting room and says to the receptionist, 'I'd like to see the doctor.'

'What seems to be the problem, sir?' asks the girl.

'There's something wrong with my penis,' he exclaims.

The receptionist, somewhat shocked and angered, says to the old man, 'You shouldn't come into a crowded waiting room and say something like that – it is most embarrassing.'

'Well, you asked me what was wrong and I just told you,' says the old guy.

'Well you could have at least come in and said there was something wrong with your ear or something, and discussed the real problem with the doctor in private.'

With that, the old gentleman walks out and comes back in a few minutes later.

The receptionist, now smiling very smugly, looks up and says, 'Yes?'

'There's something wrong with my *ear*,' says the old bloke, very pointedly.

'And just exactly what is wrong with your *ear* sir?'

'I can't piss out of it!' replies the old guy.

Seen in 'Wanted To Sell' section of newspaper.
For Sale. Complete set of *Encyclopedia Britannica*.
Excellent condition. $1000 or nearest offer. Got married
last week. Wife knows f###ing everything!

An extremely handsome man decided that it was his
God-given responsibility to marry a perfect woman
in order that they would produce children beyond
compare. After searching fruitlessly for many months, he
met a farmer who had three stunningly beautiful
daughters who took his breath away. Explaining his
mission to the farmer, he asked permission to marry one
of them. The farmer said that would be OK but he must
date each one in turn first.

After dating the first daughter, the farmer asked for his
opinion.

'Well,' said the handsome man, 'she's just a weeeee bit
– not that you'd hardly notice – err, pigeon-toed.'

The farmer nodded knowingly and suggested that
maybe he should date the second daughter. The next day,
the farmer asked how that date went.

'Well,' said the handsome man, 'she's just a weeeee bit
– not that you could hardly tell – err, cross-eyed.'

The farmer again nodded knowingly and suggested his
third daughter might be the girl of his dreams.

The next morning, the handsome guy rushed in and
exclaimed, 'She's perfect, just perfect! She's the girl I want.
May I have her hand in marriage?'

The farmer consented and they were married the next day.

Months later, a baby arrives. On visiting the hospital, the handsome guy is mortified to find the baby is the ugliest, most horrible, pathetic human being he's ever seen. He rushes back to the farmer and asks how such a terrible thing could happen, given the good looks of the parents.

'Ah well,' says the farmer, 'she was a weeeee bit – not that you could hardly tell – err, pregnant, when you proposed.'

Little girl asks her mother, 'Mummy, may I take the dog for a walk around the block?'

'No,' says Mummy. 'Because Mandy is on heat at the moment.'

'What does that mean?' asks the daughter.

'Go and ask your father,' says the mother.

The little girl goes to her Dad's workshop out back and says, 'Dad, I want to take Mandy for a walk in the park. I asked Mummy but she said the dog was on heat and that I should ask you.'

'Bring Mandy over here,' says Dad, as he takes a rag and soaks it in petrol. He scrubs the dog's backside with the rag.

'OK, you can go now, but keep Mandy on a leash and only go around the block once.'

The little girl leaves but is back a few minutes later minus the dog and the leash.

'Where's Mandy?' asks Dad.

'Well,' replies the little girl, 'Mandy ran out of petrol half-way around the block and there's another dog pushing her home.'

Paddy and Sean playing golf one day. They come to a par three with a blind-tee shot. Both tee off and watch their respective balls sail towards the flag. On reaching the green, they discover one of the balls perched right on the edge of the cup and the other is in the cup. As fate would have it, they're both playing Titleist #5s. The inevitable argument ensues, so they both decide to let the club pro sort it out. The pro walks back to the hole with them, looks at the ball on the green and then the ball in the hole. He turns to Paddy and Sean in disgust and says, 'OK. Which one of you is playing the white ball and who's playing the orange one?'

Businessman arrives home and says to his wife, 'Darling, I don't know how to tell you this, but the business I've been running for the past 40 years has gone belly up and we're broke.'

'Oh no we're not,' says his wife. 'Get into the car. Let's go for a drive into town.'

'How can you think about going for a drive at a time like this?' says the perplexed husband.

His wife insists, so they go for a drive into town. When they get there, his wife says, 'See that building? We own that.'

The husband is not only amazed but thinks that, on top of everything else in his life turning pear-shaped, his wife has gone crazy as well. They drive on.

'See that block of luxury apartments? We own those too,' she says.

'Darling, I know you're under a lot of stress at the moment, but what makes you think we own all that property?' he asks, trying to be as tactful and sympathetic as he possibly can.

'Sweetheart, remember when we first got married and, as a joke, every time we had sex you'd give me $5? Well, I kept that money and invested it. Forty years later, this is what it's amounted to. Pretty good investment, huh?'

To which the husband replies, 'Crikey darling! If I'd known you were this good with money, I would have given you all my business!'

Four women discussing their respective sons and how successful they had become.

The first woman says, 'My son is so successful, he gave a friend an apartment overlooking Sydney Harbour.'

The second woman says, 'Well my son is so successful, he gave a friend two Porsches.'

The third woman, not wishing to be outdone says, 'My son is doing so well that he gave his friend 10,000 BHP shares.'

'And what about your son, Beatrice?' asks one of the fourth woman.

'Oh he's doing very well indeed. I'm proud to say he's gay and his last three boyfriends gave him an apartment, two Porsches and a portfolio of BHP shares.'

Bloke on holiday in Africa, driving along, comes across a golf course. Being an avid golfer, he decides to call in to see if he can get a game. The pro tells him it won't be a problem, but he insists that he must use one of the local caddies.

So they set off and everything is going great until, on the 3rd fairway, a lion rushes out of the jungle towards the golfer. The caddie pulls out a shotgun and shoots the lion dead just before he reaches them.

'Thanks! I can see why the pro insisted on my taking you along,' exclaims the golfer to the caddie.

Moving on, they approach the 10th tee when all of a sudden a leopard leaps out of the bush at him. Once again the caddie pulls out his rifle and shoots the big cat dead just in the nick of time. Again, the golfer is very grateful and they move on.

They're now on the 15th green. The golfer is about to putt, when suddenly a crocodile lunges out of a nearby swamp and bites off his right leg.

Writhing in agony, the golfer screams at the caddie, 'Why didn't you shoot the bloody thing?'

The caddie replies, 'I'm sorry sir, but you don't get a shot on this hole.'

Old Sister Bernadette wasn't feeling very well, so Mother Superior called in the local doctor. After examining her, he suggested she be given three shots of whisky a day to make her feel more relaxed.

Never one to have partaken of any worldly pleasures, the old nun indignantly refused. But the Mother Superior knew that Sister Bernadette loved milk and instructed the kitchen to spike her drink on a daily basis.

Eventually, old age caught up with Sister Bernadette and, on her death bed, with her fellow nuns gathered around, Mother Superior asked, 'Sister Bernadette, are there any words of wisdom you want to leave us with before you go?'

'Yes,' said the dying nun, 'don't sell that bloody cow.'

A man and his gorilla are sitting in the clubhouse when Greg Norman walks in.

'Hey Greg,' says the gorilla's owner, 'I'll bet you $500 per hole my gorilla can play better golf than you.'

Never one to knock back a challenge, Greg says, 'You're on, buddy,' and they head off to the first tee.

The first hole is a par four over a large lake. Greg tees up and smacks a magnificent drive, 300 metres down the middle, chipping distance from the green.

'Nice shot,' says the gorilla's owner.

The gorilla then tees up, booms a drive 420 metres and straight into the hole.

Amazed, Greg picks up his ball and they move on to the next hole, a picturesque par five along a creek, slight dog-leg left.

The gorilla, who now has the honour, tees up and booms yet another drive, drawing it beautifully left onto the green, six inches from the pin.

Humiliated, Greg concedes and gives the gorilla's owner his $1000. Back in the clubhouse, Greg says to the owner, 'I've never seen anyone drive a ball so far. But tell me, since he aced the first hole and I conceded the match before finishing the second, I never got to see how he putts.'

'Oh,' says the owner pocketing his winnings, 'exactly the same way he drives.'

Paddy O'Reilly at the races one day notices a priest go into the stables with one of the owners. Curious, he follows them and watches as the clergyman blesses a beautiful thoroughbred horse. Later in the day, the horse wins its race by a country mile.

After observing this phenomenon for a few days, he

begins betting only on horses he sees being blessed by the priest. After a few weeks of successful punting, Paddy decides to put his entire life savings on a long shot he sees being blessed by the priest. You guessed it. The nag comes in stone motherless last. Paddy is devastated – he's ruined.

Seeking out the priest, he begs him to tell him what went wrong.

'Are you a Catholic or a Protestant?' asks the priest.

'Protestant,' says Paddy. 'Why?'

'Well,' says the priest, 'if you were a Catholic you'd have known the difference between a Blessing and the Last Rites.'

M y wife was telling me that it's a proven fact that men, on average, use about 15,000 words a day, whereas women use 30,000 words per day because they have to repeat everything they say.

'Pardon?' I said.

M r Bigshot, a businessman, walks into a bank in New York City and asks to see a loans officer. He says he has to go to Europe on business for a couple of weeks and needs to borrow $5000. The officer explains that the bank would require some kind of security for such a loan. The businessman hands over the keys to a brand new Rolls Royce that's parked at the kerb in front of the bank. The loan details check out, and the bank agrees to accept the car as collateral. A bank employee drives the Roller into the bank's underground garage and parks it there.

Two weeks later, the businessman returns, repays the $5000 and the interest, which comes to $15.60. The loans officer says, 'We're very happy to have been able to do business with you Mr Bigshot, and the transaction has worked out very nicely. But we're a little puzzled. While you were away, we checked you out and found out that you're a multi-millionaire. Why would you bother borrowing $5000?'

Mr Bigshot replies, 'Where else in New York can I park my car securely undercover for two weeks for 15 bucks?'

A well-dressed young bloke walks into a trendy wine bar in the heart of the city and orders a glass of ice-cold Chardonnay. The bartender obliges and places a small dish of mixed nuts in front of him. As he lifts the glass to his lips, he hears a voice commenting on his appearance: 'I say, that's a very nice suit, and such a smart tie too.'

Baffled, the young bloke looks around the bar, and establishes that he's completely alone.

'Lovely shoes too, sir,' adds the mystery voice. 'And I do like that very chic Rolex watch you're wearing.'

Perplexed, the young man beckons the bartender over and asks him if he too can hear voices.

'Oh yes, all the time, sir,' says the bartender. 'It's the nuts – they're *complimentary*.'

Young fellow pops into a supermarket to pick up a couple of bottles of Coke. He notices a little old lady following him around and staring at him. He thinks nothing of it until he gets to the checkout, whereupon the old lady pushes in front of him.

'I'm sorry if my staring at you has made you feel uncomfortable. It's just that you remind me very much of my son, who's been serving in East Timor for the past few months, and I miss him very, very much.'

'I'm very sorry,' says the young man. 'Is there anything I can do for you?'

'As a matter of fact you can,' she says. 'As I'm leaving, could you say "Goodbye Mum!"? It would make me feel so much better.'

'Not a problem,' replies the young man.

As the little old lady leaves, he calls out, 'Goodbye Mum!'

As he puts his two bottles of Coke through the checkout, the attendant says, 'That'll be $128.50 thanks.'

'Hang on!' he says. 'How can that be? I only bought two bottles of Coke.'

The attendant replies, 'Your Mum said you'd pay for her stuff!'

A bloke walks into a brothel and tells the madam he wants six girls for the evening. The next morning, as he staggers down the stairs and fishes for his wallet, the madam informs him there'll be no charge. Extremely happy and amazed, he leaves.

A couple of days later, he's back and again orders another six ladies for the evening. The next morning, he's presented with a bill for $1500.

'Hang on a minute!' he says. 'I don't get it. Last Tuesday it was free!'

'Ah yes,' says the madam, 'but Tuesdays we go out live on the Internet.'

Sherlock Holmes and Dr Watson on a camping trip. After a good meal and a very pleasant bottle of wine they retire for the night. After sleeping for some hours, Holmes awakes and nudges Watson.

'Watson, look up at the sky and tell me what you see.'

Watson replies, 'I see millions and millions of stars.'

'What does that tell you?' asks Sherlock.

'Well Holmes, it tells me that there are millions of galaxies and potentially billions of planets. I observe that Saturn is in Leo and that the time is approximately 3.30am. What does it tell you?'

'Watson, you dickhead! It tells me some bastard has stolen our bloody tent!'

Jack and Jim were down on their luck. One hot day, desperate for a long, cool beer, they checked out their combined wealth, which came to the princely sum of 50 cents.

Jack says, 'Hey Jim, I've just come up with a brilliant strategy. Give me the 50 cents and I'll show you how we can drink for free all day.'

Jack goes into a butcher's shop and buys a Bratwurst sausage, which he hangs out of Jim's fly. They walk into a bar and order two beers. Before paying the bartender, they down the drinks as quickly as they can. Suddenly, Jack drops to his knees and starts sucking the Bratwurst sausage hanging out of Jim's pants.

'You filthy perverts!' screams the bartender. 'Get the hell out of my hotel!' and boots them out the door.

They continue the scam all day, visiting about 25 pubs in all.

'I can't do this any more,' moans Jack, 'my knees are getting really sore from all the kneeling.'

'You're sore!' replies Jim. 'I lost the Bratwurst sausage 20 hotels ago!'

Bloke walks into a pub and orders a glass of beer. After taking one sip, he throws the rest into the barman's face. Flabbergasted, the barman asks, 'What the hell did you do that for?'

The drinker apologises profusely, 'I'm really sorry. I've had this compulsion to throw beer over bartenders for years. I can't tell you how embarrassing it is.'

The barman says, 'Look mate, I reckon you ought to see my psychoanalyst. He's treated my brother and sister for compulsive disorders and he really is very good. I've got his number here, give him a ring and get back to me after you've seen him.'

The grateful drinker thanks the barman and leaves. Several months later, he's back in the bar.

'Great to see you back,' says the bartender, serving him up a beer. 'Did you go and see my shrink?'

'I certainly did. He was great. I've been seeing him twice a week for the past month and I think he's fixed my problem,' says the drinker taking a sip of beer and then promptly throwing the remainder into the barman's face.

'Hang on,' sputters the barman, wiping the beer from his face with a towel, 'the doctor doesn't seem to have done you much good.'

'On the contrary,' says the customer, 'he's done me the world of good.'

'But you threw the beer in my face again!' the barman exclaims.

'Yes,' said the drinker. 'But it doesn't embarrass me any more.'

B loke on a tram with a baby under each arm.
'What lovely babies,' says an elderly woman. 'What are they? Boys or girls?'

'Dunno,' says the bloke.

'Well, what are their names then?' inquires the old lady.

'Dunno.'

'Really!' says the old lady. 'What kind of a father are you?'

'Look lady,' replies the bloke, 'I'm not their father. I work for a condom company and these are two complaints I'm taking back to the factory.'

The day after his Master's triumph, Tiger Woods attempts to enter a very exclusive, snooty golf club. He's stopped at the gate by a burly security guard.

'I'm sorry, sir, but we don't allow black people in here. However, if you'd like to get a game, there's an excellent public course about a 3 wood down the road.'

Tiger responds, 'But I'm Tiger Woods!'

'I do apologise Mr Woods,' replies the guard. 'I didn't recognise you, sir. In that case, it's an easy 7 iron down the road.'

God and the Devil decided to play a round of golf one day, just for the fun of it. The Devil won the honour on the first hole and teed off with a perfect 270-metre drive right down the middle. God then teed up and hit a very ugly hook that headed straight out of bounds into the trees. The ball bounced off one tree and then another, flew high into the air back towards the fairway, landing on the back of a passing seagull. The seagull carried the ball towards the green 380 metres away. Unfortunately, the ball slipped off the bird's back into a lake just short of the green. No sooner had the ball landed in the lake, when a giant water spout rose and elevated the ball into the air, onto the green and into the hole.

The Devil put his hands on his hips, looked at God and said, 'Now look, do you want to play golf or just fart-arse around?'

Dad comes home from work and asks Mum where his son is.

'In the garage playing with his new chemistry set,' says Mum.

As Dad's walking towards the garage, he hears a banging noise and, upon opening the door, sees his son pounding a nail into the wall.

'Hang on, son, Mum told me you were playing with your new chemistry set. Why are you banging that nail into the wall?'

His son replies, 'Dad, it's not a nail, it's a worm. I just put these chemicals on it and it became hard.'

His Dad gets very excited and says, 'Tell you what son, give me those chemicals and I'll give you a brand new Volkswagen.'

Quite naturally, the son agrees.

The very next day, the son goes into the garage and sees parked in the garage a brand new Mercedes. Just then, his Dad walks in.

'Where's the Volkswagen?' asks the son.

'Right there behind your Merc.'

'Where did the Merc come from?' asks the son.

'It's a gift from your mother!' replies Dad.

A vicar is visiting an elderly parishioner, Mrs Johnson, one afternoon. He is invited into her living room for a cup of tea. While she's out getting a couple of iced Vo-Vos, the vicar notices an electronic Hammond organ standing in the corner with a bowl of water on top. On closer inspection, he notices a condom floating in it. On Mrs Johnson's return, he remarks, 'Could you explain this unusual ornament please?'

'Oh yes Reverend,' she replies. 'Isn't it wonderful? I was walking through the park last autumn and found this little package. It said to put it on your organ, keep it wet, and it would prevent disease. And you know I think it's working! I haven't had a cold all winter.'

Elderly couple, having trouble remembering things, decide to see their doctor about it. After the consultation, he suggests that they start writing things down to help them remember. Later that night, while watching TV, the old man gets up from his chair.

'Where are you going dear?' asks his wife.

'To the kitchen,' he replies.

'Will you get me a bowl of ice-cream?'

'Sure,' he says.

'Maybe you should write it down like the doctor said.'

'Don't worry love, I'll remember,' he says.

'Well, I'd like some strawberries on top,' she says. 'But you'd better write it down because you know you'll forget.'

'I can remember that!' he says, now becoming a tad impatient. 'You want a bowl of ice-cream with strawberries on top – right?'

'I'd also like some whipped cream as well,' she says. 'Now for goodness sake, write it down as I know you'll forget.'

Hopping mad now, he says, 'I don't need to write that down! I'll remember just fine!' Fuming, he heads off to the kitchen.

After about 15 minutes, he returns from the kitchen and hands her a plate of bacon and eggs. Staring at the plate for a moment she says, 'You forgot the toast!'

Same old guy, driving home from his bowls club's annual Christmas lunch, answers the car phone. He hears his wife's voice sounding very distressed and urgently warning him, 'Claude, I've just heard on the radio there's a car going the wrong way on the South Eastern Freeway. Please be careful!'

'Hey,' says Claude, 'not just one car Beryl. There's hundreds of the buggers!'

Bloke standing in front of the lion enclosure at the zoo is astonished to see one lion at the back of the cage furiously licking the bum of another lion. Calling over an attendant, he asked if the lion was sick or something.

'Oh no, sir,' says the attendant. 'A group of lawyers came through about an hour ago. One of them fell into the enclosure and the lion ate him. He's just trying to get the taste out of his mouth.'

Bloke comes home from work one day to find his wife waiting at the front door with several suitcases packed.

'Where do you think you're going?' he asks.

'To Surfers Paradise,' she says. 'I've just found out that I can make $400 a night doing what I give you for free.'

'Hang on a minute,' he says, and disappears inside and returns a few minutes later with his suitcase packed.

'So where do you think you're going?' she asks.

'I'm going with you.'

'Why?' she asks.

'I just want to see how you're going to live on $800 a year,' he replies.

A few days before a proctological examination, a one-eyed patient accidentally swallows his glass eye. He rings his regular GP who tells him not to worry, nature would take its course in due time. At the proctologist's office, the patient undresses and bends over. Of course, the first thing the specialist sees when he looks up there is the glass eye staring back at him.

'You know Mr Price,' says the doctor, 'you're really going to have to learn to trust me.'

A man comes home unexpectedly to find his wife in the bedroom in front of a mirror caressing her breasts.

'Why are you fondling your breasts like that?' he asks.

'I went to the doctor today and he told me that I have the breasts of a 25-year-old,' she proudly proclaims.

The husband says, 'Oh yeah. And did he say anything about your 52-year-old arse?'

'Oh no darling, we didn't talk about you at all.'

A priest gets a haircut. When it comes time to pay, the barber says, 'I cannot accept money from you, for you are a good man – you do God's work.' The next morning the barber finds a dozen Bibles at the door of his shop.

A pharmacist comes to the barber for a haircut, and again the barber refuses payment saying, 'I cannot accept money from you, for you are a good man – you help sick people with your drugs. The next morning he finds a dozen packets of jelly-beans and a year's supply of aspirin at the door of his shop.

A lawyer comes in for a haircut, and again the barber refuses payment saying, 'I cannot accept money from you, for you are a good man – you serve the justice system.' The next morning, the barber finds a dozen lawyers waiting for a haircut.

Ninety-year-old codger walks into his doctor's office and asks for a prescription for some Viagra.

'No problem, Mr Mansfield,' says the doctor. 'How many do you want?'

'Just a few,' he replies. 'Maybe six, but cut each one into four pieces,' he says.

'That won't do you any good,' says the doctor.

'Oh, I don't need them for sex. I just need them so my old fella will stick out far enough so I don't pee on my shoes.'

Little old lady walks into a grubby café and orders a hamburger. The waitress yells out to the big burly cook behind the counter, 'One hamburger!'

With that, the cook grabs a hunk of minced steak, stuffs it under his bare armpit, pumps his arm a couple of times to squeeze it flat then tosses it on the grill.

'That's the most disgusting thing I've ever seen,' says the old lady.

'Just be thankful you didn't order a do-nut,' whispers the waitress.

Farmer sitting at the bar of a country pub with a black eye and abrasions.

Barman: 'How'd you get the black eye Fred?'

Fred: 'Some things you just can't explain Harry.'

Barman: 'Try me.'

Fred: 'Well, this morning I was milking Bessie the cow and, just as the bucket got full, she kicked it over with her left leg. So I tied her leg to the post on the left of the stall.'

Barman: 'No big deal – what happened then?'

Fred: 'Some things you just can't explain.'

Barman: 'I'm still listening Harry – what happened then?'

Fred: 'Well, I sat down and started milking her again and, just as the bucket got full again, she kicked it over with her right leg. So I tied that leg to the left post of the stall.'

Barman: 'Then what happened?'

Fred: 'I sat down and started milking again when the

stupid cow knocked over the bucket with her tail.'

Barman: 'But you still haven't told me how you got the black eye and bruises.'

Fred: 'Well, I ran out of rope so I took off my belt to tie Bessie's tail to the rafter. That's when my pants fell down – just as the missus walked in. As I said Harry – some things you just can't explain.'

A lawyer walks into his client's cell on death row and says, 'I've got some good news and bad news for you Leroy.'

Leroy says, 'OK. What's the bad news?'

'The bad news is that your last appeal has failed and there won't be a stay of execution.'

'That's terrible!' says Leroy. 'What could possibly be the good news then?'

'I got your voltage reduced.'

Mr Isaacson picks up his young son Aaron from school.

'So son, how was school today?' asks Dad.

'Really great, father, I got a part in the school play.'

'Oh really?' says the father. 'What part did they give you?'

'I'm playing the part of a man who's been married for 25 years.'

'Don't worry son,' says the father, 'maybe next year you'll get a speaking role.'

Drunk flops down next to a priest on a bus and starts reading a newspaper. After a few stops, the drunk leans over to the priest and slurs, 'Hey Father, what causes arthritis?'

The priest, not wanting to pass up an opportunity to admonish this disgusting miscreant replies, 'My son, it is caused by loose living, being with cheap, vile, wicked women, too much alcohol, and a contempt for your fellow man.'

'Crikey!' mutters the drunk, returning to his paper.

The priest, feeling a little guilty at having been so hard on the drunk, apologises. 'I'm very sorry. I was a little harsh and unsympathetic just then. How long have you had arthritis?' he asks.

'Oh it's not me, Father. I was just reading here that the Pope's got it.'

Husband reading a book and wife watching television. She says, 'Darling, if I died tomorrow, would you get married again?'

'Sweetheart, we've had a very happy marriage and I

know you'd want me to be happy again – of course I would. How about you?'

'Well yes, I think so. But would you let your new wife wear my dresses?'

'Of course I would darling. It would be a shame to let all those beautiful clothes go to waste,' says the husband.

Some time goes by as he continues to read and she watches television.

'Darling,' she starts again, 'would you let her wear my shoes?'

'Yes,' he replies. 'And for the same reason. It would be a shame to throw away all those expensive shoes.'

He goes back to his book and she to her telly.

'Darling?' she says, renewing the inquisition, 'would you let her use my new Ping golf clubs?'

'Don't be stupid!' he says without thinking. 'She's left handed.'

Priest visiting an old lady in hospital. As he sits down, he spies a bowl of nuts on the unit beside the bed.

'Mind if I have a few?' he asks.

'Not at all,' the old girl replies.

They chat for over an hour and as the priest stands to leave, he realises that instead of eating just a few peanuts, he's actually emptied the bowl.

'I'm so sorry, Mrs Smithers, I seem to have eaten all your nuts,' he says sheepishly.

'Oh that's all right Father,' she replies. 'Ever since I lost my teeth, all I can do is suck the chocolate off them anyway.'

Three sons of a Yiddish Mama left their homeland, went abroad with each one of them making their own, individual fortunes. Some years later, they meet to discuss what they sent their mother as thanks for bringing them up to be such successful businessmen.

The oldest son, Moishe, says, 'I built a huge 50-room house for our mother.'

The middle son, Abraham, says, 'I sent her a Mercedes with a driver.'

David, the youngest, says, 'Remember how Mama enjoyed reading the Bible? Well, now that her eyesight is failing, I sent her the most remarkable parrot. It can recite the whole Bible. Mama just has to name the chapter and verse and the parrot recites it perfectly – the only one of its kind in the world.'

Not long after, a letter of gratitude arrives from their mother.

'Moishe, the house you built is too large, I only live in one room as it takes me weeks to clean.

'Abraham, I am too old to travel and the chauffeur not only talks too much, he has appalling body odour.

'David, the chicken was delicious!'

Husband and wife driving to the weekly kennel club meeting when, in the middle of the road, they see this beautiful, big green frog. Being animal lovers, the husband brakes suddenly stopping just inches from the frog. He gets out of the car, gently picks up the frog and places him on the side of the road.

'Why thank you,' says the frog.

Astonished, the husband exclaims, 'Well I'll be blowed! A talking frog!'

'Not just a talking one, mate, but a magic one as well,' says the frog. 'And, after that wonderful act of kindness, I'm going to grant you one wish.'

The husband says, 'In that case, I wish for my dog to win this year's Blue Ribbon event at the Annual Kelpie Show.'

'Not a problem,' says the frog. 'Let's take a look at him.'

With that, the owner gives a whistle and out of the car jumps this ugly, mangy old three-legged kelpie. The frog takes one look and says, 'Look pal, I may be a magic frog but there are some things in life beyond my special power. Sorry, but have you got another wish?'

The husband thinks for a minute and says, 'Actually yes. I wish that my wife would win the next Miss Universe contest.'

As his wife gets out of the car and approaches them, the frog says to the husband, 'Give us another look at the dog?'

Bloke sitting quietly reading the paper one Sunday morning when 'Clang!' – he is knocked senseless by his wife who is now standing over him holding a very large frying pan,

'What the hell was *that* for?' he says.

'I found a piece of paper in your trouser pocket with "Betsy" written on it,' she replies.

'Oh darling,' says the husband, regaining a little of his composure, 'don't you remember a couple of weeks ago I went to the races? Betsy was the name of a horse I bet on.'

The wife, satisfied with the explanation, apologises for whacking him.

Three days later, he's again sitting quietly reading the paper when 'Clang' – he's bonked over the head again.

'What's *that* for this time?' he says.

'The *horse* rang this afternoon.'

Bloke walks into a bar with his dog. Barman says, 'You can't bring that dog in here, it's against the health regulations.'

'But hang on,' says the bloke, 'this ain't no ordinary dog, this is a talking dog.'

'Bulldust!' says the barman. 'If that dog can talk, I'll give you $100.'

'You're on,' says the owner, putting the dog on a stool. He asks the dog, 'What do you find on top of a house?'

'ROOF!' says the dog.

'Correct. Now, what do you find on the outside of a tree?'

'BARK!' says the dog.

'Very good. Now, who is the greatest baseball player of all time?'

'RUTH!' says the dog.

'Well,' says the dog's owner, 'I guess you've heard enough. I'll take that hundred in 20-dollar notes thanks.'

The furious barman hands over the money and tosses man and dog out into the street. As they pick themselves up off the footpath, the dog says to his owner, 'Do you think I should have said Dimaggio?'

A Rabbi was seated next to a Methodist minister on an aeroplane. Just after take-off, the flight attendant came around for drink orders.

The Rabbi said, 'I'll have a gin and tonic with a squeeze of lemon thanks, miss.'

The attendant then asked the minister if he'd also like a drink.

Indignantly, the Methodist minister said, 'Young lady, before I would permit any alcohol to pass my lips, I'd rather commit adultery!'

'Hold my order!' said the Rabbi. 'I didn't realise there was a choice.'

Bloke arrives at his grandparent's farm and notices his grandad sitting in his favourite rocking chair on the front porch, naked from the waist down.

'Grandpa, what are you doing?' he exclaims.

'Well Timmy,' says Grandpa, with a faraway look in his eyes, 'last week I was sitting out here with no top on and I got a stiff neck. This was Grandma's idea.'

Kids in Sunday School. The teacher asks where they think Jesus is at this very moment.

Young Stephen raises his hand and says, 'Please Miss, he's in Heaven.'

'Very good,' says the teacher. 'Yes, Natalie, where do you think Jesus is?'

'Please Miss, he's in my heart every day Miss,' says little Natalie.

'Now Johnny, you've been very quiet. Where do you think Jesus is?' asks the teacher.

'He's in our bathroom Miss,' says Johnny.

'In your bathroom? How do you know this?' asks the teacher.

'Well Miss, every morning when my Dad gets up, I hear him banging on the bathroom door and yelling, "Jesus Christ! Are you still in there?"'

Isaac and Rebecca are celebrating their 50th wedding anniversary when Isaac says to Rebecca, 'Darling, I was just wondering, have you ever cheated on me?'

'Oh Zack, how could you ask such a question now,' says Rebecca, 'on this of all nights?'

'I really need to know Becky – please.'

'Well alright, since you're being so insistent – three times,' she sighs.

'Three times!' he exclaims. 'When?'

'Well, Zack, remember when you were 32 and you really wanted to start that business on your own and the bank manager wouldn't approve the loan? Remember when he then personally came over to the house and just signed all the papers – no questions asked?'

'Oh, Becky, you did that for me? I respect you more than ever. So when was number two?' he asks.

'Well, Zack, remember when you had that heart attack and you were needing that very tricky operation and no surgeon would touch you? Remember how Dr De Groot flew all the way out from South Africa to do the surgery himself and you've been in great shape ever since?'

'I can't believe this! Rebecca, you should do such a thing for me. You saved my life – I couldn't wish for a more wonderful wife. All right then, when was the third time?' he asks.

'Well, Zack, remember a few years ago, when you were running for President of our golf club and you were thirteen votes short . . . ?'

Bloke meets a girl in a bar and, after a few drinks, they start to get a bit friendly.

He says, 'Hey, let's go back to my apartment. Whaddya say?'

She says, 'That'd be great. Do you have cable?'

'Nah,' he replies, 'but I've got some rope and a couple of old ties that might get the job done.'

Little-known facts about Mahatma Gandhi:
• He walked barefoot everywhere.
• As a result, his feet became thick and hard.
• He was also a very spiritual person.
• When he went on a hunger strike he became quite thin and frail.
• Due to his enforced dieting, he ended up with very bad breath.

Thus, since that day forth he has been known as:

'The Super Calloused Fragile Mystic Plagued With Halitosis.'

(You may groan here)

A young female teacher writing up a lesson on the blackboard for her Grade 6 students. Having to start at the top of the blackboard, she has to really stretch up.

Suddenly she hears a giggle coming from the back of the room. Turning around quickly, she asks, 'What's so funny Patrick?'

'Well, Miss, while you were stretching, I just saw one of your garters.'

'You dirty little boy!' she yells. 'Get out of my classroom and don't come back for at least three days.'

Turning back to the blackboard, she realises she hasn't titled the lesson and has to reach up even higher. Again, there's an even louder giggle.

'What's so funny William?'

'Well Miss, I just saw both your garters.'

Again she yells in anger, 'You're even worse than Patrick. Your punishment is going to be even worse. Get out of my classroom and I don't want to see your face for three weeks.'

By now she's very embarrassed and flustered, and, in her confusion, drops the blackboard eraser on the floor, whereupon there is another burst of laughter. Looking around quickly, she sees little Johnny heading for the door with his school case in his hand.

'Where do you think you're going?' she asks.

'Well Miss,' says Johnny, 'judging from what I just saw, I reckon my school days are over!'

Bloke having a drink in a very dark bar. He leans over to a rather large woman sitting next to him in the gloom and says, 'Hey, do you wanna hear a very funny blonde joke?'

The woman replies, 'Well yes – but, before you tell that joke I'd better warn you – I happen to be a blonde, I'm six foot tall, weigh 110 kilos, and I'm a professional athlete and body builder. The blonde sitting next to me is six foot two, weighs 120 kilos, and is an ex-professional wrestler. Next to her is another blonde who's six foot five, weighs 125 kilos, and is the current National Kick Boxing Champion. Now, do you still want to tell that blonde joke?'

The bloke thinks about it for a moment and says, 'Nah, not if I'm going to have to explain it three times!'

Midget goes to his doctor to complain that his testicles have been aching for years and he's finally come to do something about them. The doctor tells him to get up on the examination table and lie on his back. Once he's up there, the doctor pulls down the midget's trousers, places a finger under his left testicle and gets him to cough.

'Aha!' says the doctor, as he places his finger under the right testicle and gets his patient to cough again.

'Hmmmm,' he says. 'I think I can see what the problem is. Nurse, bring me in a pair of very sharp surgical scissors will you.'

The nurse brings in the scissors. The doctor tells his now terrified patient to just lie there and keep looking at the ceiling and that, 'This won't hurt a bit.' All the midget hears is snip, snip, snip on the right side and then snip, snip, snip on the left side.

'OK Mr Small, you can get off the table, pull your pants up and let's see if the operation was a success.'

The midget is delighted as he walks around the doctor's surgery – for the first time in years, his balls don't ache.

'Doc, this is a bloody miracle! My balls have stopped aching! How the hell did you do it?' cries the delighted patient.

'Simple really,' says the doctor. 'I just cut two inches off the top of your cowboy boots.'

B loke walks into a bar and orders a beer.

'Thank you sir, that'll be one cent thanks,' says the guy behind the bar.

'One cent?' exclaims the drinker.

'Correct sir, one cent. Is there anything else I can get you?'

'Well yes. I'd like a big, fat, juicy T-bone, medium rare with lots of chips and vegetables thanks.'

'Certainly sir, that comes to five cents,' says the bloke behind the counter.

'Hang on, hang on,' says the drinker, 'that's ridiculous. Where's the bloke who owns the joint?'

'Oh him,' says the barman, 'he's upstairs with my missus.'

'What's he doing with your wife?' asks the customer.

'Same thing I'm doing to his business,' replies the barman.

A married couple are dining at a very swanky restaurant when a beautiful, statuesque redhead walks over to their table, exchanges a warm, friendly kiss and a hug with the husband and then walks off.

'Who was that?' demands the wife.

'Darling, I can't hide it from you any longer – the deception is killing me. That young lady is my mistress,' says the distraught husband.

'Your mistress? Well, that's it Arthur! I want a divorce!' fumes the wife.

The husband looks her straight in the eye and says, 'Are sure you want to give up that penthouse in Surfers Paradise, the Mercedes Sports, your furs, your jewellery and that very fat portfolio of BHP shares?'

For quite some time they continue their meal in silence. Suddenly, the woman nudges her husband and says, 'Isn't that Stephen over there? Who's he with?'

'That's *his* mistress,' replies the husband.

'Oh,' she says, taking a sip of her wine, 'she's not as cute as ours.'

A t the end of the job interview, the interviewer asked the young, 18-year-old, VCE graduate, fresh out of school, 'Now Nathan, what sort of salary were you looking at?'

The young man responded confidently, 'Well, something in the neighbourhood of $150,000 a year, depending on the benefits package.'

The personnel officer leaned back in his chair with his hands behind his head and said, 'What would you say to a benefits package of ten weeks' annual leave, two fully paid overseas holidays per year, full medical and dental benefits, 50,000 company shares that you can cash in at any time and a company car – say a Mercedes 500 SEL?'

The young man sat bolt upright with his mouth wide open and said, 'Wow! Are you kidding?'

'Of course,' said the interviewer. 'But hey, you started it!'

Three mothers sitting on the beach in Surfers Paradise each talking about how much their sons love them.

Sadie says, 'You know that Arthur Boyd painting hanging in my living room? My son, Arnold, bought that for me for my 75th birthday. What a good boy he is, and how much does he love his mother.'

Minnie says, 'You call that love? You know that Jaguar I got for Mother's Day? That's from my son, Bernie. What a doll!'

Moira says, 'That's nothing. You know my son, Harvey? He's in therapy with one of Australia's top psychoanalysts in Collins Street. Five sessions a week, at $500 each. And who does he talk about? Me!'

Aussie tourist walks into an Irish pub and sits at the bar to have a pint. All of a sudden a bloke yells out, 'Number 47!', and all the other drinkers start falling about laughing.

A few minutes later, another bloke yells out, 'Number 77!' and again everybody starts laughing hysterically.

'What's going on here?' the Aussie asks the barman.

'Well, it's like this, sir. These fellas have been drinking here for years and they all tell the same jokes. So a couple of years ago, we decided to give all the jokes numbers so if you knew what the joke was, you'd just yell out the number and if they think it's funny, they laugh. Saves an awful lot of time sir.'

The Aussie thought he might give it a try himself so, after waiting until it was all quiet, he stood up and shouted, 'Number 89!'

Well, the whole bar started laughing hysterically for more than ten minutes, tears streaming down their faces and holding their sides. The pub was in uproar.

'So tell me,' says the Aussie, 'how come they laughed more at my joke than the others.'

'Two reasons, sir,' says the barman. 'Firstly, it was a very funny joke, and secondly, they hadn't heard it before.'

Bloke walks into his local Post Office one morning and spies a short, middle-aged, balding man with glasses standing at the counter methodically putting cards in pink envelopes, sealing them with little red heart stickers and then spraying each one from a large bottle of perfume. Finally, curiosity gets the better of him and the bloke walks up to the balding man and asks him what he's doing.

The man says, 'Oh I'm sending out 1000 Valentine's Day cards signed "Guess Who?".'

'But why?' asks the bloke.

'I'm a divorce lawyer,' says the balding man.

John Blackman
Aussie Gags

My grandfather died peacefully in his sleep. Which is more than I can say for the three passengers he had in his car at the time.

At school, John Blackman was voted the student most likely to recede. Despite this, he has emerged as one of our best-loved funny men. In *Aussie Gags*, the king of the backhanders presents a collection of over 1400 of his favourite one-liners and jokes.

It was so cold today, I saw a politician with his hand in his own pocket.

Ever wished you could come up with an unforgettable one-liner at a crucial moment? Or be known as the king or queen of jokes? This is the definitive book of jokes from all over the world that make Aussies laugh.

John Blackman
Aussie Slang

If you don't buy this book you're one chop short of a barbecue!

Is your knowledge of Aussie slang sadly lacking? Are you feeling like a bandicoot on a burnt ridge, running around like a blue-arsed fly? If so, don't chuck a wobbly, simply take a squiz at *Aussie Slang* and she'll be apples!

This literary triumph from John Blackman is the ultimate guide to the lingo of Down Under. Blackman defines all the great slang and phrases that confront everyone, every day, all around Australia. Where words are inadequate, talented cartoonist Andrew Fyfe has let his dark, fertile mind run rife with illustrations.

So take a Captain Cook at this little bottler, impress the world with your grasp of the Aussie vernacular and find a special place (preferably one that doesn't flush) for this masterpiece in your house.

Previously published as John Blackman's *Best of Aussie Slang*

Richard Stubbs
Still Life

Legendary stand-up comedian, hugely successful radio
breakfast and TV host, Richard Stubbs, is now available in
a handy take-home pack. *Still Life* is a hilarious collection of
Richard's musings on life in general. Journey with Richard
as he helps you with . . .

Timeless advice to new parents . . .

'Think of babies as being like your pissed mates. They are,
in fact, very similar. Like your pissed mates, babies make
no sense when they talk, they can't walk without your help
and they may throw up at any moment. I don't know about
you but I've had years of experience dealing with people
like that.'

Your sexuality . . .

'One memorable down moment I thought I'd brighten my
day by doing the latest *Cleo* quiz: "Are You A Lesbian? Take
Our Quiz and Find Out!" Sure enough it turned out I was.
Oh, I should have known – all the signs were there. I've
always been attracted to women and indeed openly live in a
sexual relationship with one . . . I'd just never looked at the
big picture before!'

With characteristic fast-paced and caustic wit, Richard navi-
gates a hilarious course through his own life experiences
with unputdownable results. If you thought Jerry Seinfeld's
SeinLanguage was funny, watch out – *Still Life* will prove
fatal for anyone wanting a quiet journey while reading on
public transport.

David Dale
The 100 Things We Loved About the 20th Century

The 21st century is another country . . . we'll do things differently there. But in our journey from the 20th century we will need to take some souvenirs – a small amount of carry-on baggage to remind us of the way we were.

In this book, David Dale analyses those essential souvenirs – the ideas, products, people, fads and entertainments that changed Australia during the past 100 years. From the Pill to the poker machine; from *Number 96* to *Friends*; from Germaine Greer to Paul Hogan; from the Mars Bar to the Big Mac; from Daffy Duck to Indiana Jones; from the Walkman to the Internet . . . these are the things that captured the imagination of Australians on their trip to a new millennium.